making gardens works of art

making gardens works of art

works of art

creating your own personal paradise

keeyla meadows

SASQUATCH BOOKS
SEATTLE

Published by Sasquatch Books
Printed in Singapore by Star Standard Industries Pte Ltd
Distributed in Canada by Raincoast Books, Ltd.
08 07 06 05 04 03 02   6 5 4 3 2 1

Cover and interior design: Karen Schober
Copy editor: Rebecca Pepper

All photographs by the author. Page 1: Glazed ceramic pot with *Thalictrum*.
Pages 2–3: Painted steel "Butterfly Bench" with blue *Salvia guaranitica* and *Sisyrinchium*.
Pages 5–6: Ranunculus. Page 128: Clematis 'Henry'.

Library of Congress Cataloging in Publication Data
Meadows, Keeyla.
        Making gardens works of art : creating your personal paradise / Keeyla Meadows.
            p. cm.
        ISBN 1-57061-307-9 (alk. paper)
        Gardens—Design. I. Title.

        SB473.M388 2002
                712'.6—dc21   2001049657

Sasquatch Books
615 Second Avenue
Seattle, Washington 98104
(206) 467-4300
www.SasquatchBooks.com
books@SasquatchBooks.com

*This book is dedicated to the
Garden and to all those who go there to enjoy the fruits of the land
and to lend a hand in creating paradise here on Earth.
It is further dedicated to gardening and dancing friends; to Dave Radlauer,
for loving and faithful partnership in creating this book, tireless editorial attention,
and the willingness to grow; and to two paradisaical cats, Bix and Jelly.*

contents

acknowledgments

As with creating a garden, making a book is a collaborative process, and there are many people that I'd like to acknowledge and extend appreciation to. Jennie McDonald, my editor, has been an invaluable guide in every phase and aspect of making this book; it's been a pleasure sharing this journey with her. All the folks at Sasquatch Books have tuned into the spirit of adventure that has guided this project. I thank Gary Luke, Joan Gregory, and Aley Mills.

I'd like to extend my deepest thanks to Chris Owens Gaspich for her inspired graphic design of the original proposal for *Making Gardens Works of Art*, and to Karen Schober at Sasquatch Books for her thorough realization of the book design, her expert handling of the complicated job of integrating photographs and text, and for her uniquely artistic eye in presenting garden imagery.

There are several people who offered support and input in the early stages of the book, including Ann Leyhe and Erin Conner with photo selection, and Katherine Pritchett, Chiori Santiago, and Chris Cosgrove with writing. As with my garden shows, I'd like to acknowledge the excellent work of all the fabricators who are also independent artists: my brother, Dan Howard, for design collaboration on Sonja's gate; Lawrence Gandsey for garden furniture; Patrick Fitz-Gerald for the morning glory arch; Stan Huncilman for copper sculpture and bronze armatures; Rod Fitiausi for ceramics; and Mussi ArtWorks Foundry for creative support and excellent craftship of all the bronze sculpture.

All of my clients have been a pleasure to work with on their gardens and have been generous in making their gardens available to me to photograph and write about. I extend my warmest appreciation to my landscape crew Ronald Menjivar, Andres Munoz, and Julio Reyes, with special thanks to Julio Escobar, Landscape Supervisor, who has stuck with the business and details of making gardens works of art for over ten years. Katey Carter, the business and gallery manager for Keeyla Meadows Gardens and Art, is a consistent asset to our garden ventures.

My special thanks go to Lou Trousdale and Alex Marchel at American Soil Products and to the many wonderful and invaluable plant growers and nurseries up and down the West Coast. I'd also like to thank the editors, writers, and photographers at the various magazines that have published articles about my garden, as well as the crew for *Grow It!* Leslie Lucas, with the San Francisco Flower and Garden Show, has also given invaluable support. for making creative gardens.

My garden roots took hold in my family home, and I'd like to thank my mother for imparting her love of the garden, sweetpeas, columbine, daffodils, fruits and vegetables, and the color yellow. Thanks to my father for supplying me with my first cameras; to my sister-in-law Virginia for setting an example of photographing everything; and to my "Grandpa" Dave for setting me on a path of colorful vision headed for a garden paradise.

Left: *Glazed ceramic pot and stepping stones, with white clematis and Scotch moss.*

Right top and center: Euphorbia martinii.

The garden is an extraordinary place to explore the arts, to expand what gardens can be, and to extend the boundaries of what we think of as the garden space. For me, it is a place to play with colors and shapes, to follow my enthusiasms. I compose my gardens as an artist composes a painting, with an eye to creating a complete and unified scene that is inviting and satisfying to view and travel through. It is a creative process involving trial and error, arranging and rearranging, with inspiration as my guide. I invite

introduction: be an artist in your garden

you to join me on this winding path, with a few unexpected twists and turns along the way.

I'm lucky to have found a way to combine my love of gardening with my training in art. I studied art at the University of California at Berkeley, where I received a masters degree in sculpture. Working with clients for more than twenty years in many challenging and rewarding garden environments has given me a wide range of experiences to share with you. I have led many garden classes and workshops. My home garden and those of my clients have been included on numerous garden tours and been given wide exposure in magazines such as *Sunset, Horticulture, Fine Gardening, Organic Gardening, Metropolitan Home,* and *Traditional Home,* as well as in several magazines overseas.

Below: *Glazed ceramic sculpture "Garden Gladys," with pink tiger lilies.*

Below right: Malus floribunda, *flowering crabapple tree.*

Far right: *Bronze sculpture "Garden Gladys," with purple heucheras.*

Before I began designing my garden, I spent a lot of time studying the paintings of Claude Monet, looking at photos of the master surveying his garden and setting up his easel and canvas at his chosen vantage points. I saw that he would plant himself at one end of a scene, so that everything in his view would become the painting. Everything he saw, although it was three-dimensional, would be flattened out on his canvas as strokes of paint representing light and color.

Imagining how Monet painted in the garden changed how I saw gardens and gardening. I realized that the garden could be turned into a collection of scenes for the artist to paint—or, in my case, to photograph. This means that you can "look" in your imagination for all the pictures in your garden and then set about making them.

Taking this idea, I set up my garden as if I were planning to paint it from several angles. I found that this made my garden very photogenic, that each angle of the garden had all the elements needed to make a complete composition.

I believe that an appealing garden composition has much in common with successful drawing or painting:

- ❋ It needs a strong *focal point*—a tree, plant, bench, planter, fountain, sculpture, or other feature.
- ❋ The focal object should interact with its setting, bringing into play whatever is around it.
- ❋ Shapes and colors should interact through *harmony and contrast* to organize the space.

Above left: *Sculpture detail with water droplet.*

Left: *Painted chair with dahlias.*

Right: *Closed eye of "Women of Paradise" ceramic pot, as viewed through 'Orange Emperor' tulips.*

Above: *Gouache on paper "Gardeners at Sunset."*

Left: *Gouache on paper "Gardeners with Tools."*

To create my compositions, I use design techniques such as pulling colors through a visual field, using lines that direct attention up or down, near or far, and varying the elevation. All of these techniques serve to move your eye through space or invite your eye to linger on detail and texture. Also, the explosion of plant varieties and the broad spectrum of materials available today call upon us to be increasingly inventive, to add personal touches, and to celebrate the garden's wonders with fresh voices.

Throughout this book I talk with you just as though we were neighbors having a friendly chat over the garden fence. I share reliable gardening practices that guarantee your success, exploring:

❋ The magic of color
❋ The foundations of a successful garden
❋ Some fresh approaches to mapping and arranging garden spaces
❋ Creative tips for personalizing your own benches, planters, and fountains and even making your own sculpture

Above: *California poppy.*

Right: *Pink ranunculus.*

In the various "Tips" scattered throughout the book, you'll find exercises designed to develop your skills and imagination as a gardener, regardless of your level of experience. Please feel free to pick and choose the ones that seem helpful or inspirational, and use them in any order that appeals to you.

Because shovels thoroughly connect me to the garden, I've grown to love them. Shovels are the point of contact between a gardener and the earth; they're a gardener's best friend and primary tool in the real work of gardening. Throughout the book, shovels appear in text and images as both a practical tool and a symbol of artistic imagination. They represent the simple, mundane steps in the garden, which, like the strokes of a paintbrush on canvas, add up to a work of art.

As you read this book, you'll learn to carry a paintbrush along with a shovel as you turn your garden into a work of art. You'll discover ways to apply the principles and techniques used by artists to create your own unique garden compositions. My hope is that at the journey's end, you will find yourself a more independent and artistic gardener.

Below: *Painted shovels with aluminum tubing near* Tagetes lemmonii.

Right: *"Planted" painted shovels.*

It can take a long time to find the right starting point for a garden. But once you find it, everything comes together like magic. Equally important is having the confidence to create a firm foundation where your design ideas can grow. To get started, let's see how to look at the garden as a work of art.

What Makes a Garden a Work of Art?

I approach garden design from an artist's perspective. While it is currently popular to look at garden spaces as rooms, I begin the design process with a blank canvas, as I would a sculpture or painting. I want

getting started on the artist's path

to create a garden painting: a vision that is gorgeous to view, intriguing to talk about, and inviting to enter.

Preceding pages, left to right: *Glazed ceramic sunflower. Sunflower and blue sky. Blue ceramic sunflower.*

Left: *Copper and steel cone with mixed succulents.*

Below: *Leaf detail on planter.*

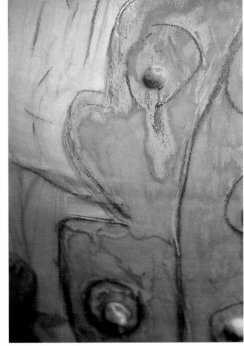

Seeing your garden as a blank canvas will open up new possibilities for experimentation and fun—with livable results. In this book I show you how to cultivate an artistic eye, hand, and imagination. You'll discover that with a wave of your magic wand you can transform ordinary garden features such as benches, arches, trellises, and pathways into artistic elements of a garden painting.

Your garden adventure has unlimited points of departure. You can follow Alice into Wonderland by making small things big and big things small. Think of something that you see every day and then, in your imagination, enlarge it ten times, one hundred times, and even larger. Follow Dorothy over the rainbow by planting figures of tin or straw. You could make an emerald garden or one in blue and pink, as I did. You might get wild and venture into Jurassic Park. The world's treasure trove of art and artifacts is at your fingertips. What is your inspiration for a uniquely personal garden?

You don't have to be an artist to let artistic inspiration guide you in garden design. However, you do need to meet the challenges of your garden projects with enthusiasm, passion, and gusto. So let's dig in.

Above: *Swiss chard 'Bright Lights'.*

Right: *Notebook with glazed ceramic tile and flowers.*

Tip: Stretch Your Imagination

Here are some ways to stretch your imagination or visualize original garden creations:

- Visit a museum or the art section of a bookstore.
- Select a painting and take time to really absorb the elements of its composition, taking notes.
- Find a color that looks good enough to turn into an ice cream cone or to use to paint a bench. Write down a description of it.
- Find an animal shape that would make a fun gate, such as a cat.

Once your imagination is warmed up, go a few steps further:

- On a piece of paper, write down the name of a basic garden feature, such as bench, trellis, arch, or gate.
- Cut or tear pictures of that feature from magazines, and paste them on the paper.
- Buy a few postcards of paintings or art that you like.
- Cut these images into pieces.
- Be imaginative when you paste the artistic imagery on or next to the feature.

The point of this exercise is to help you visualize an original garden feature by combining artistic imagery with an everyday object.

- Now take one object that captures your attention, something you see daily—like a piggy bank—and use it as a design idea for five features in your garden.
- You may want to use a photocopier or your personal computer to craft your creation: you can change the color, make it larger or smaller, or change the shape. Add these images to your notebook or design folder.
- Find a way to stretch your imagination every day.

Starting Points

I love getting started on new garden projects. I find adventure and excitement in breaking new ground and planting seeds, feeling the air marking a new season, inviting new ideas into the garden. Having a starting point when addressing the design aspects of your garden is a crucial garden tool that you'll come to rely on as you do a favorite trowel.

When I became fully committed to making gardens into art, I began looking for new paths to explore in the garden. I imagined myself opening my garden gate and inviting in some of the great artists of the past who loved the garden. One of these was impressionist painter Claude Monet. Light from the sky as it interacts with plants and water is always a key element in Monet's art. It was from Monet that I learned to look at the sky as part of the overall garden picture.

Beginning with the very simple starting point of light from the sky, I turned the garden in the back of my house into a living picture. Blue morning glories had taken off for the sky from the fence at the back of my garden, carrying my imagination with them. The lovely starry flowers became the inspiration for a copper morning glory arch that is the centerpiece of my garden. The color of the morning glories mirroring the blue of the sky became a major starting point for several garden features in a symphony of blues, including blue paving tiles, a blue bench, blue pots, blue ceramic wall caps, and blue flowers. The blues all came together in a wonderful painting that included the sky.

Left: *Morning glories climbing on copper arch.*

Above: *Mixed paving, and planter with* Clematis *'Duchess of Albany'.*

Right: Phacelia.

The evening sunset was the starting point for the west-facing garden in front of my house. I chose fiery colors that reflect the setting sun—salmon-colored rocks, and plants in yellow and orange: fuchsia-tinted watsonia, 'Princess Irene' tulips, and coral roses. A ceramic pot, glazed and planted in sunset colors, is joined by a 7-foot copper sculpture of two women, one holding up a fish, which draws your attention skyward. From across the street, the elements blend together into a garden painting, connecting earth and sky.

With or without a visit from Monet, you can easily think of your garden as a work of art to stretch your imagination. Any theme can be translated into a garden object. Toys, kitchen tools, sports gear, pets, giant silhouettes from drive-in movies, ancient petroglyphs—all are fair game for garden design. Once, for instance, in an Alice-in-Wonderland mood, I decided to make a giant crayon and turn it into a fountain.

When you're getting started, a single focusing idea is a crucial design principle. I find this works for all levels of design, from creating complex gate and lighting projects to choosing a collection of bulbs for a single pot. Having a starting point brings focus to your design. Starting points are the seeds of ideas that, when well nourished, spring forth into inventive garden designs.

Left: *Closed tulip.*

Far left, below: *Copper sculpture "Two Women with Magic Fish."*

Right: *Glazed ceramic pot with Lillian Austin rose near melon lilies.*

Below: *Parrot tulip.*

Left: *Painted blue petal bench with morning glory flower.*

Above right: *Variegated-leaf strawberry.*

Right: *Notebook with leaves.*

Following pages: *Surface detail of steel and colored cement sculpture.*

So that I won't lose these seedling ideas, I keep several notebooks handy. Because I'm always working on at least one garden design, I may have a notebook for each new area of my garden, or one for each of my clients' gardens. I like to put these notebook ideas into the Alice-in-Wonderland part of my imagination, where images can double, triple, or even quadruple in size or shrink until they're as small as a penny. Keeping my imagination tuned to Alice in Wonderland, I'll play with each image on my internal imagination screen, enlarging it, shrinking it, changing its color. Then I'll have the various images play with each other, merging and combining into one.

Here's an example: I saw some luscious strawberries at the farmers market. Fruits always inspire me. I love strawberries, both to eat and to look at. So I made a doodle of a strawberry in my notebook. Since making that first doodle, I have drawn strawberries on planters, molded them in clay, and even enlarged them for a seat and a sculpture. I have also found several varieties of strawberry plants that I wasn't previously aware of, and I'm constantly on the lookout for more, gathering the ingredients for my "Wild Strawberries!" garden.

Stretching your imagination is as important an exercise as taking walks to keep your back and limbs in shape for the hard digging and lifting that gardening requires. Imagination is an important aspect of the design side of gardening. I find that spending time browsing in a bookstore stimulates my imagination and inspires me to stretch, reaching for new ideas and images.

Just as important as selecting a starting point for designs is developing a firm foundation for your garden. When I say "foundation," I'm talking about the three elements essential to the growth of plants: soil, water, and light. Getting a firm handle on these will free you to play with the creative and imaginative aspects of gardening.

Soil Is the Foundation

The question people ask most often when they come into my garden is,

foundations: let's talk dirt, water, and light

"How long have you lived here?" What they are really asking is, "Can I have a garden like this?" People imagine that

Preceding pages, left to right: *Spring planting of tulips and heucheras.* Tulipa viridiflora *'Greenland'. Peony tulip 'Lilac Perfection'.*

Left: *Artichoke flower.*

Far left: *Painted wall with glazed tile cap and spring-blooming ranunculus and linaria.*

Below left: *Notebook with paint chips and flowers.*

Below: *Detail of bronzed sculpture "Music Girl."*

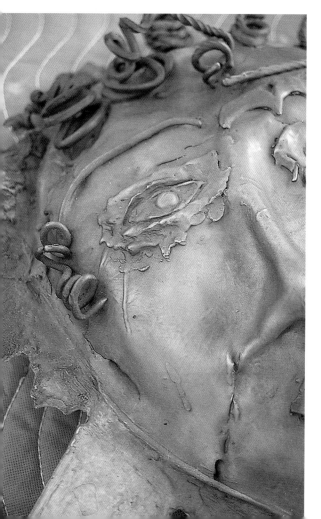

it takes a long time and great effort to have a dream garden. My answer is that a wonderful garden is not necessarily a matter of time or experience but of having a proper foundation. Everything depends on dirt. A great garden, one that is a pleasure to work in, relies on a firm foundation—in other words, soil. Good soil, in which plantings will thrive and look great no matter what.

Let me tell you a story.

It was a chilly November morning, and a committee of women had gathered in my demolished backyard. These ladies did not look happy, and I understood why. My garden was to be included in a big fund-raising tour of "secret" gardens, and all they saw before them was an expanse of dirt.

"What did you do to the garden, Keeyla?" they asked anxiously. "How are you going to have a show garden by April?" they added. "Don't worry, don't worry, don't worry," I assured them, borrowing a line from a Yoko Ono song. I had a secret that would give me a garden by spring.

In April, as the date of the garden tour approached, the committee women's frowns turned to smiles when they walked into my garden and were greeted by a sea of tulips, ranunculus, Iceland poppies, coral bells, and giant bleeding hearts. More than a green thumb was at work here, and the women wanted to know my secret.

What was the secret? Let me whisper it in your ear: my special soil mix. Yes, the right mix works miracles in a very short time. Never underestimate the power of dirt. It's the essential foundation of a successful garden. My recipe for soil mix took my garden from zero to a thousand blooms in five months. (See the Tip on the next page for my secret soil mix recipe.)

The point of this story is dirt—garden soil, to be precise. A wonderful garden depends on a proper foundation. Plants thrive best in soil with air in it so that their roots can grow freely. Clay soil holds water. Roots get stuck in clay, and it doesn't drain well, becoming mucky and discouraging root growth. Very sandy soil often lacks nutrients and can support only a very limited range of plants.

We marvel at how plants in nature have adapted to every conceivable kind of soil and weather. But a garden needs soil that supports a wide variety of plants. A foundation of loose and nutritious soil encourages quick growth for nearly any plant. Still, it can't be just any dirt; it's got to be great dirt!

It's important to understand the type or types of soil you have in your garden. For instance, I have swampy conditions on one side of my garden, rich, loamy soil in the center, and heavy clay in the front. You will need to get out in your garden with a shovel and investigate. Is the soil loose and sandy or hard and compacted? You might even map the soil conditions in your garden—an exercise that will help you decide what and where to add amendments. Put a garden soil map into your notebook.

Connie's garden is another testament to the quick results my soil mix can guarantee. Connie called me one day in April. Her back garden was beautiful, but the front yard was an eyesore. She couldn't bear to host another Fourth of July block party with this sad patch of weeds staring at her!

We didn't have much time, but I had faith in my soil mix. We mounded it in the planting areas and filled containers with it. By the time of the Fourth of July block party, her garden was radiant—all dressed up in yellow, lime, and white flowers and foliage. Everyone wanted to know what had made the plants grow so fast. But I kept it to myself . . . until now.

I came up with my soil mix because I was often disappointed with the bulk soil mixes available. These are often low in organic matter and tend to be either too sandy or too heavy. However, most soil suppliers have been willing to make a custom mix that meets my needs.

I first developed this soil as a container mix, which is generally lighter than a garden mix. One fall, however, I began using it in the garden when planting bulbs, and the result was spectacular.

Tip: Keeyla's Secret Soil Mix

Here is my secret recipe for soil that is both light and nutritious; it encourages root growth, provides quick drainage, and reduces overall maintenance. For Keeyla's Secret Soil Mix, combine:

3 parts chicken manure and rice hull mix

1 part red lava rock: size $5/16$-inch clean (dust-free or pebble-like)

1 part red lava rock: size $5/16$-inch minus (or less), grit-like

1 part screened loamy sand

2 parts fir bark: size $1/8$-inch minus (or less)

2 parts well-composted organic matter

The organic matter can be well-composted material from your garden (such as leaves and grass clippings), or eco compost (recycled tree clippings), or a commercial organic amendment. Red lava is an essential ingredient because it lightens the soil and allows air to penetrate, thus encouraging quick root growth and ensuring good drainage. Chicken manure and rice hulls, and the organic matter, provide rich nutrition.

Before ordering enough of this mix to redo your whole garden, try mixing up a sample batch to test in container plantings. You'll want to fine-tune the recipe to accommodate climatic conditions in your region. For example, in dry areas, you may want to use less lava rock for a slightly heavier mix that will hold more water.

For general plantings, blend this mix with the existing soil, making well-fortified plant beds about 8 inches deep. If you experiment with varying proportions of mix to existing dirt, you will find a blend that works well for your local soil conditions and weather.

Ask your supplier or nursery to help you locate the ingredients to perfect your own mix. And ask whether they can order the materials in bulk, which can substantially lower your costs.

After experimenting with my special mix in bulb plantings, I became very adventurous and started adding large quantities of it to most garden sites. Digging out or mounding up whole beds 4 to 12 inches deep is now a standard part of my planting procedure when preparing a new garden.

Water Play

When people learn that I'm a gardener, they often ask, "How can I get my plants to do better?" First I tell them the story of my secret soil mix, and then I suggest they learn what I call "deep watering"—which leads to a story about Joe the gardener.

Joe, our family gardener, was Italian and didn't talk much. He looked like a movie star, and although I was too young—just six years old then—to have a crush, I followed him around like a puppy. I learned from him that watering was a time to be quiet and to tune in to plants.

Although we had an irrigation system, Joe spent hours lugging heavy hoses around the property, directing the flow of water with his thumb to each individual plant. Somehow he had learned to respond to a thirst in plants that could not be quenched by an irrigation system. Following Joe around our garden, I became aware of each plant: the large, spreading leaves of aralia, fringed in yellow felt, or the crinkled purple flesh of the creeping ajuga. Joe's quiet way taught me to take the time to discover what each plant needs, whether it be fertilizing, pruning, or watering.

Deep watering can also be a time to let the garden nurture you. Water decants the fragrance of the earth. A sprinkler on the lawn accentuates the sweetness of fresh-cut grass. Watering is a way to immerse yourself in the luxurious embrace a garden offers. At the same time, you'll find yourself getting to know and appreciate your plants better as they grow and change through the seasons. Like Joe the gardener, I use my thumb to water, I take plenty of time, and I give the garden my full attention—especially with spring bulbs, such as tulips and daffodils.

As a landscaping contractor, however, I would not install a garden without an irrigation system; here in the West, irrigation systems are essential. But I still recommend hand watering as a way to become more intimate with your garden.

Sometimes hand watering brings me a wistfully pleasant childhood memory. On one side of our family's garden, a fence became the trellis for an annual crop of sweet peas, but the vines were just out of reach of the lawn sprinklers. So I made it my job to set out the seeds each spring and water them. I'd haul the hose out onto the lawn, drag it in the direction of my seed bed, and run back and turn on the water, the pressure forcing the long, green tube to dance like a gyrating snake.

Running out to catch the waving hose, I'd thrust the nozzle up, spraying water skyward only to be drenched in a rain of diamond droplets. I made great sheets of diamond droplets spinning through space, quenching my little girl's thirst to create something.

Left: *Bronze wall fountain with six water spouts.*

Right: *Self-portrait, watering.*

Below: *Keeyla watering like Joe the gardener—with thumb.*

Today I cherish that sweet memory of what I call my "diamond water paintings." Perhaps when you're hand watering—even in these days of fully automated
irrigation—you too might find some childhood memory or inspiration of your
own, whether it's a renewed connection to earth, sky, and water; fresh creativity;
or a release of blocked energy. Bounce water off the leaves; watch the earth drink
up the water.

The point of watering is to get the roots wet. All the advice I can give you adds
up to making sure that water penetrates down through the soil into the plant's
root system. This can be accomplished through hand watering, spray irrigation, or
a drip system. Watering for 2 to 15 minutes every day will keep the top layer of
soil slightly moist so that water can easily reach the roots. This gives glorious
results and can easily be accomplished with a drip system. At a minimum (if you
don't water every day) I recommend watering planting beds for 20 minutes three
times a week, planted containers every other day, and trees at least once a week.

If you water less frequently, you may need to break up the ground surface with a
trowel and add mulch so that the top layer of soil does not become compacted. You
may also need to water longer to ensure that water is soaking through to the roots.

Light rain does not soak the roots. If winter rains are light in your area, or if
there hasn't been significant rain for ten days, check to see whether you need to
water. You can easily do this by digging down around the plant roots to see if the
soil is wet or dry.

Irrigation systems help to guarantee that your garden is getting sufficient water.
Modern systems use clocks to deliver adequate and efficiently budgeted moisture.
I always put drip systems on container plantings set to drip at least 2 minutes daily.

Many clock-driven systems operate with a "water budget" so that in hot weather
you can punch up the budget, adding 10 percent, 25 percent, or 50 percent more
water, and in wet weather you can easily reduce it. This ability also helps during
droughts, or when you are encouraged or required to reduce water consumption.

I prefer drip irrigation systems to spray irrigation for flower beds for several
reasons. They deliver water more economically, directly to the soil. Drip systems
are simpler and cheaper to install, move, or extend, and they are also gentler on
plants. The force of a spray can knock flowering plants down or soak delicate
blooms, spoiling them. I use spray systems for lawns and occasionally for larger
planting beds.

One caution about drip systems is that they are somewhat fragile and can be
punctured when you are digging or turning soil in plant beds. So keep a repair

Above: *Bronze crayon fountain.*

Right: *Detail of bronze crayon fountain.*

Far right: *Detail of small fountain.*

kit handy with connectors, goof plugs (plugs for unwanted holes in tubing), and spare ¼-inch tubing and emitters.

Light

Light is a key element that is often overlooked in the garden. You want to consider both the aesthetics of light and the practical aspect of providing your plants with the amount of light they require.

The garden invites us to become observers of light, to marvel at the powerful feeling of light illuminating the surface of a leaf or flower petal so that it appears to be on fire. Have you noticed that the light of spring shimmers through the translucent, light green colors of new growth, whereas summer light reflects off the harder surfaces of summer foliage? An object that blends with its surroundings in spring light might appear to stand alone in the glare of summer light, when it contrasts more deeply with the dark shadows. So, when designing your garden, consider how it engages light through the seasons.

For example, you could plant a grape arbor that casts appealing shadows of leaves and fruits onto a nearby wall in the summer light. Paint the wall in two colors, setting the background for a silhouette bouquet. Another way to work with shadows is to place rocks so that a chorus of flower shadows dance on them.

While most flowers require sun for full vitality, many varieties grow best in the shade. Most nurseries organize perennial flowers, annual flowers, and shrubs by their light requirements, keeping the sun-loving plants in the sun and shading the ones that prefer more shade.

Deep shade, particularly the compacted areas beneath trees, where low-growing plants can't get their roots into the ground to gather nutrients, is one of the more difficult situations. When you're planting in deep shade, pay extra attention to the soil, mounding up as much light soil mix as possible. You can also see whether trees can be pruned or removed: extensive tree work is often needed overhead before you can garden below. Inspect trees annually and trim them when needed to maintain a balance of light for your shrubs, perennials, and ground covers.

Most nursery plant labels indicate the light requirements for that plant. While I generally recommend an experimental approach to gardening, this is one area where I tend to go by the book. Sun lovers love sun, and shade lovers do best in shade. I have found, however, that lightening the soil with Keeyla's Secret Soil Mix allows me to grow sun-loving bulbs such as tulips and daffodils in deeper shade than is possible in heavier soils. For the most reliable results, though,

Above: *Bronze "Crayon Head" fountain.*

Above right: *Olympic poppy.*

Far right: *Tulip shadows.*

I suggest you stick with the nursery's recommendations for light conditions.

Leaf color can indicate the amount of light a plant needs. Most plants with gray-green leaves are sun lovers. Incidentally, many plants with this coloring, such as lavenders, sages, and artemisia, are drought-tolerant. The gray coloration is an adaptation to strong sun. Plants with tender leaves, such as coleus, impatiens, and begonia, prefer shade and will burn if planted in the sun.

If your garden has more sun than you want, you can plant trees. Many of the trees that will provide instant shade, such as oaks, maples, and olive trees, are available in 2-, 3-, and 5-foot boxes. While you'll pay quite a bit more than you would for 5- to 15-gallon trees, you'll achieve the desired effect much more quickly. Landscape contractors can help you find and install mature trees suited to your needs. It's well worth the cost to bring good-sized trees into a barren garden to jump-start a shade canopy for people and plants. I've found olive trees that were being removed from orchards and have successfully relocated them to clients' gardens. In the right climate, olives are hardy and long-lived, and provide moderate shade.

Once when I was eight, I came home to find the hallway to my bedroom door lined with fourteen cartons. "Has the circus come to town?" I wanted to know. I opened all the cartons and found myself surrounded by a sea of paper flowers. My grandfather must have bought out the paper flower market on his trip to Mexico! Yellow and orange life-sized sunflowers, red and pink ranunculus, turquoise and lavender plate-sized dahlias; this was just the beginning of the flower parade that came out of those boxes. Sitting on my bed, I imagined that I was wearing a

the magic of working with color

skirt made of every kind of colored flower. Flowers. I love flowers. I love flowers. *I love flowers!*

Having a Vision of Paradise

My grandfather had given me my first vision of paradise: flowers and colors. Having such a vision of paradise is easy if you begin with flowers and colors as starting points, especially for garden projects. The colors of a single petal of a 'Fantasy' Parrot tulip, with its marbled pinks and greens, could generate a color scheme for painting a planter or a mural on a garage wall.

Flowers and their annual greetings are the well-earned bounty of the gardener. Gardening with flowers ignited my passion for color, turning me into a painter and transforming how I create gardens. Color is at the center of my vision of a garden paradise. Color—subtle, bold, electric, or simply gorgeous—is a great starting point for design.

Learning to work the colors and textures of plants and flowers into the hardscape—benches, paths, fountains, and containers, for instance—develops the design process further. Harmonizing your garden features with plant colors brings flowers *up close and personal!* One thing I don't mind having in my face is a flower.

As you learn to blend the colors of plants and the hardscape, your own personal vision of paradise will begin to emerge. Soon you'll be able to put on a show with flowers that will bring an audience to its feet. Bravo for the flowers! Bravo for colors!

Preceding pages, left to right: *Glazed handmade ceramic tiles and house paint. Shirley poppy. Tulip and glazed pot.*

Left: *A chorus of tulips.*

Above: *'Fantasy' Parrot tulip.*

Right: *Mexican paper flower.*

Harmony and Contrast

In and out of the garden, color is a vehicle for joy. To enter into the world of color, simply let your eyes linger on things. Take time to notice the subtle shades of green on a single leaf or the patterned wing of a butterfly. For a lesson in color, examine a single flower. Look at the mixture of colors in the center. Or try looking at several petals of a flower. They will often have many shades of one color. The 'Fantasy' Parrot tulip petal is a good example, with shades of pink ranging from a bright, saturated hue to a soft pastel. Take several pink tulips, pink ranunculus, and pink poppies, and you will have a palette of harmonious pinks.

Looking closer at the tulip petal, you'll see contrasting lines and splotches of green mixed in with the pink. The Viridiflora tulip 'Groenland' also has this marvelous coloring. The harmonious pinks bring a smooth kind of pleasure, like major chords in music, while the green adds contrast, spice, a feeling of exuberance. Keep the two principles of *harmony* and *contrast* in mind as you practice with color, and you will gain confidence in making bold color statements. I use color chips from a paint store to illustrate these principles, and I often have an envelope of color chips in my purse for some project that I'm working on (see the Tip on page 52).

Color has a life of its own in the garden. A planting of white, yellow, or orange tulips seems to actually shed a glow of light on the surrounding area, even tinting the air that you breathe. The yellow of a daffodil planting appears to tint the light between the individual flowers. Imagine inhaling air infused with an ambrosia-scented light. With the daffodils I marvel at how this odd little bulb that looks like an onion will flower into a yellow trumpet calling out the return of the sun to my garden in spring.

I've found that I can enrich and intensify this perception of color by adding containers, furnishings, painted walls, or natural stones with colors that harmonize with the flowers and foliage. Whole areas of a garden will "read" or be seen as a color.

You can create a sense of motion in the garden by making pathways of a single color. As the eye is drawn from flower to stone to wall along the path, the color seems to flow. I call this the "Yellow Brick Road effect." End the path by placing a focal feature—like the Emerald City of Oz—where the eye can come to rest.

One of my clients, Sonja, loves yellow—the bright, sunny yellow of a new day. In Sonja's garden, we wove yellows through the landscape. In addition to planting an all-yellow rose garden, we dug yellow-leafed carex behind rocks, planted Dahlberg daisies and daffodils along steps, and stuffed a planter with yellow Iceland poppies and flowering bulbs. We treated the house to a makeover simply by repainting the window frames and an entrance gate yellow.

Far left: *Harmony in colors of Provence, with* Rosa *'Lady Banks'.*

Left: *Painted steel gate.*

Below left: *Blue "flame" chairs, glazed pot with clematis, and painted window frames.*

Right: *Glazed tile bench back with Provence fabric cushions.*

Below: *Glazed ceramic handmade tile wall fountain with* Clematis montana *var.* rubens.

Sonja's garden is only a short walk from the sparkling Pacific Ocean, so we chose blue for contrast with the yellow: light and sea. The gateway to her entry is designed with a nautical motif. On the entry wall we installed a fountain with fish. The ocean inspired a mural with the flying fish, and I designed yellow tiles for the bench backs, completing our homage to light and sea.

Coloring Your House

I have learned to look at the house as part of the garden. Your house is a major component of your garden, and it often needs some new features or painting as part of your project.

I look at all the colors of a house and compare them to the colors that are in the garden. Do you want to extend the colors of your house into the garden? Or add some colors from the garden to the house? Sometimes you can make a simple change by painting the front door or the window frames. Brightly glazed tile, a piece of art on a wall, a fountain can add color highlights. Planted containers in entryways are always inviting and enhance the colors of your house.

Color can transform your house. But watch out! It can also transform your life,

Left: *Painted chair.*

Below: *Laura's house and patio before and after.*

as it did for Laura. Laura is a red lady—a modern wild woman doing cartwheels in her capoeira class (a blend of Brazilian dance and martial arts). She began our garden consultation by saying, "My house is the biggest thing in my garden, and it's boring."

We looked up at her gray house. I opened a book of paint color chips, saying, "Choose five colors." She drew them as if from a deck of tarot cards. No surprise: They were all bright. This house no longer had a place to hide. It would have grown feet and run if it could. Its life as just another gray house in a gray neighborhood was over. We were headed for the circus. I drew my sorceress's color cape around us, declaring, "Let the transformation begin."

The house was our starting point for our color exploits. Soon we were glazing wall tiles with her children and choosing more colors for planters. By fall we were eating homegrown pomegranates that matched the colors of the custom garden furniture. Laura's friends commented that Laura herself had metamorphosed into a brilliantly colorful lady.

Above: *Handmade ceramic tiles.*

Right: *Iceland poppies and painted chair.*

Coloring Your Garden

To color your garden, choose a color *palette*. Picture in your mind the classic artist: easel, beret, smock, brushes, and . . . that odd-shaped piece of wood called an artist's palette, with daubs of paint squeezed from tubes. On it, artists create a color palette, the selection of colors used in a work of art.

In the garden you have a tremendous range of plant colors, so selecting a color palette, and working with a limited group of colors, is an important design step. You can choose any selection of colors to make up a usable palette, and that choice will bring definition to a project. A single palette can be used for a container planting, a single garden bed, or a whole garden. Remember to consider your house or other structures when creating your color palette. Coloring your garden includes seeing and working with everything that is out there: pavings, fences, the sky, surrounding trees, and structures. You are weaving the colors of all the elements into a whole picture or painting.

I have several ways to test colors to see whether they will work as well in the garden as well as they do on paper. Following the example of painter Claude Monet, I look at how the colors I've selected are affected by light. To do this, I'll put together a large bouquet of flowers in the colors I'm planning to work with and set them out in the space I'm designing.

The colors will shift throughout the day, from morning to noon, afternoon, and evening. If you try this, record how the colors change during the day. Take some photos, or even sit down with paper and paint. Matching the bouquet colors to paint on paper will help you see the colors and get more comfortable using paint on objects or in the garden. Try two bouquets of different colors to compare the effect of each.

I like color to move, so I tend to use lines or streams of color. I will take one color, such as the blue of the sky, and then mirror and move that color through the garden. In my garden, I started with blue tiles on the path. I then had the idea to make a blue tile cap for the wooden retaining wall of a raised planting bed, which I planted with blue flowers. At the end of the wall I set a blue pot. All of this could be enjoyed by taking a seat on a blue bench.

Repeating a color is often necessary for getting enough of that color into the garden to feel its presence. Rendering gardens in brilliant, exotic colors is challenging: it takes a lot of color to saturate a garden canvas.

Left: *Pair of vases with pear design.*

Above: *Ceramic vase with yellow roses and foxgloves.*

Right: *'Pipit' daffodils and 'Sweet Harmony' tulips.*

Far left: *Colored cement and steel "Calla" sculptures with petunias.*

Left: *Lime weigela and foxglove.*

Below: Tulipa viridiflora *'Greenland' and* diosma.

It helps to plant a color in all of the layers of the garden. For example, if I'm planting a white garden, I work white through a whole area, choosing whites in the ground covers, perennials, vines, and trees.

By the way, white brings a quality of elegance to any setting. But while it is an easy color to work with by itself, it can be very tricky with other colors. I find that white grates against bright colors. It can make a harsh contrast because it draws attention from other colors. If you want strong, saturated colors, don't mix them with white.

White does stand alone very well, with greens of all shades or with pastels. It's especially good in the shade, with traditional architecture, and with browns, bronzes, and eccentric greens.

To soften the light in my own garden, I used meadowlike mixed border plantings and pastels to wash the colors into one another, like an impressionist painting and to diffuse the moist spring light.

Just be aware when you are selecting color palettes for your garden that you are also engaging qualities of light. Every location has a different light, which acts differently on plants. Bougainvillea, for instance, works with strong, brilliant light, while forget-me-nots or baby-blue-eyes look like water in soft, filtered light.

Painting with Flowers

Once you have your color palette, you're ready to use a technique I call "painting with flowers." It puts the icing on the garden cake. Painting with flowers is just about the most fun you can have in the garden: planting ribbons to make moving streams of color, using harmonizing or contrasting hues, and developing a dynamic push-pull of colors in your planted beds.

In my own garden I "pulled" blue into the raised bed by using purple shades that harmonize with the blue and contrast with the yellow. Then I introduced new colors in a range of pinks that move out from the purples, meaning that they are pinks that have blue hues in them. In the raised bed across from the purples and pinks, I moved from the cooler bluer pinks into warmer pinks that have yellow and orange tints.

With these techniques, you can move colors around the garden as though you were painting on a canvas. Your garden becomes a work of art, and you become an artist painting with flowers!

Bulbs are one of the richest sources of color in the garden. Tulips offer especially saturated colors in a wide variety. This makes them useful for painting the garden. You can decide what color is needed in an area or a pot, and then look in your bulb catalog and find just the right hue to plant.

Planting bulbs in trenches can create the effect of a flowing stream, focusing light through the translucent petals of flowering bulbs.

I plant bulbs closer together than is recommended in bulb charts or books, with very good results. This method has worked well for me in numerous gardens. Gardening is an experiment; an adventurous attitude yields adventurous results.

Below: *Summer-blooming lily 'Antonia'.*

Right: *A favorite plant combination: tulips and Iceland poppies.*

Following pages: *Glazed ceramic ground sculpture "Butterfly Couple."*

Tip: Trenches for Bulb Plantings

When planting bulbs, especially tulips, daffodils, and lilies, I dig out trenches in the garden. Here's how I plant several types of bulbs in one trench:

- Dig a trench twice as deep as the diameter of the largest bulb, plus an inch or two. Make the trench from 6 inches to a foot wide, depending on how much space there is in the bed.

- Place an inch of Secret Soil Mix at the bottom of the trench.

- Sprinkle the soil mix with bulb food or bone meal.

- Lightly cover with more soil mix, and then place your bulbs. Place the larger bulbs in the trench first: lilies, daffodils, alliums.

- Add a little soil mix between these bulbs, and then interplant with medium bulbs: tulips, hyacinths, and baby gladiolus.

- Add more soil mix, and in the remaining space plant the smaller bulbs: freesias, ranunculus, ixia, ipheion, 'De Caen' anemone, tritonia, and sparaxis.

- Cover the open trench up to the existing soil level with soil mix.

- For variety, dig trenches next to each other to create two different plantings, or lightly sow the trench with wildflowers for a wild garden look. I use nemophila, poppies, linaria, two-tone nemesia, and gathered seeds such as blue flax and cornflowers. Following this recipe in the fall will set your garden up for a delightful flowering of bulbs throughout the spring and into the summer season.

I've found that shapes work very much like color, particularly if you focus on harmony and contrast. As eager as you may be to get out into the garden with a shovel, I recommend that you first organize your garden space on paper by thinking about shapes. For this activity, use your garden notebook to jot down ideas. (You'll need a large pad of lightweight drawing paper—about 14 x 17 inches—to work out a full garden space.)

Shapes

A garden consists of an assortment of shapes. Formal gardens rely on geometric shapes. Naturalistic gardens are made

a fresh look at the garden space

with organic shapes. Combining organic with geometric forms creates a strong sculptural garden composition.

An exercise I once did in a sculpture class proved to be useful when it came to designing my garden space, which is square. In that class we drew outlines of shapes on a courtyard pavement in chalk. Most of the shapes were geometric—squares, circles, and triangles—but there were a few kidney shapes as well as paisley and amoebic shapes. Then we placed various three-dimensional cardboard boxes, tubes, and round cheese crates within the outlined shapes drawn on the ground. Arranging and rearranging the cardboard boxes inside the flat outlines drawn on the pavement was a good lesson in noticing how shapes work together.

When designing my garden space, I used a variation of this exercise by covering my kitchen table with butcher paper and drawing a square on it. I gathered objects of various shapes and sizes—such as small boxes, jars, and cosmetics containers—to experiment with my garden arrangement.

Preceding pages, left to right: *Hydrangea and delphinium with mixed paving of handmade blue tiles, flagstone, and brick. Notebook with paint chips and flowers. Upright garden shovel sculpture.*

Below: *Planting of Canna and Agapanthus 'Dark Storm' by pool designed by architect Alyson Flynn.*

Right: *Chartreuse weigela.*

Surprisingly, while laying out my garden in this way, I noticed that placing an object a few feet inside the boundary line of the garden made it feel bigger. So I put an arch 10 feet inside the boundary line of the garden: it not only enhanced the space in front of it, but also created a space to discover beyond it.

Just as a color can be a starting point for an area of a garden, a shape can also make a viable starting point. You could take a circular planter, a circular table, and a circular patio, and then contrast them with a square sculpture. In Sonja's garden we made two lines of rectangles—from benches and built-in planters against perpendicular walls—that converged at a circular planter.

Using harmony and contrast, you can confidently put together a composition of shapes. Repeating a shape such as a circle in different sizes, and using varying heights and angles, will create harmony. Juxtaposing circles and squares makes for contrasts. Focusing on harmonies and contrasts in structural shapes of the garden enhances your awareness of the sculptural qualities of garden space.

Another pointer for composing with harmonious shapes in the garden is to find a shape in the existing architecture of the house and repeat that shape in the garden. For example, in Madeleine and Ivan's garden, we repeated the triangle shape of the entrance landing portico in a triangular arbor over the sidewalk garden gate. You can think of this technique as extending or pulling the lines of the house into the garden.

A variation of this technique is to repeat a shape found in the architecture and then add a new twist to it in the garden. For one garden, I designed a gate with squares of different metals and glass that harmonized with many squares found throughout the architecture. Shapes are basic units of form and can serve as building blocks for organizing garden space.

Focal Points

Now that we've talked about shapes, let's consider the garden space from the perspective of movement. We travel through the garden on several paths, sometimes walking to destinations and sometimes just sitting still while our senses do the traveling. Our ears might follow a trail of bird songs, breezes, fountains, or the urban noise of traffic. We might be drawn along fragrant airways of honeysuckle, rose, lemon, and jasmine blossoms, or our eyes might leap from sight to sight—from a spring crocus pushing through snow to glistening icicles melting on bare branches. The garden offers many treasures to savor.

Tip: Get in Shape: Flex Those Circles, Triangles, and Squares

Take a tour where you live and notice shapes in the architecture, observing the shapes of doors, windows, porticos, and rooftops. How do these shapes interact with the pathways, fences, and walls of the adjoining garden?

- Make scribble sketches in your notebook of shapes to use in designs.

- Put shapes to work in your garden. Try swirling a circle into a spiral for a brick patio design. Use squares of different sizes to make a pathway. Or bend an oval into an interesting seat.

- Play with shapes on paper. Take paper in different colors and cut it up into a variety of shapes. Draw a simple outline of your garden on a flat sheet of paper and drop the cut-out pieces onto it.

- Let chance arrange the shapes. You might find some pleasing combinations that you would not otherwise have thought of.

- Keep playing with the shapes until you find an arrangement you like. Then tape or glue them into place for reference in designing your garden.

One of my primary organizing ideas for designing garden spaces is the need for visual paths for the eye to travel. As in a connect-the-dots puzzle, the eye wants to travel along all of the points in a garden until the whole picture emerges. I call these dots, or locations, the *focal points* of the garden.

Focal points are locations where the eye naturally rests. They are the backbone of your garden composition because they indicate where you need a feature, such as a fountain, bench, or container, to direct the flow through the garden, both visually and physically. Making a map of these locations is essential to composing your garden masterpiece.

Destinations

Think of the excitement that builds when you are preparing for a trip. You can bring that same excitement into your garden by creating a destination, a spot containing a feature that you will physically travel to. Destinations are special places that you want to take friends to or that will draw you outside in all types of weather. There is joy and comfort in having familiar spots to return to, ones that make you feel rejuvenated, peaceful, whole, and happy.

Try organizing your garden around an itinerary of destinations, just as you would plan a trip. This trip could be along a rainbow trail with different color

Far left: *Painted fence, gate, and trellis with* Rosa *'Climbing Iceberg' and* Verbena bonariensis.

Below left: *Painted metal bench and planted terra-cotta pots.*

Below right: *Painted shovels "planted" near* Tagetes lemmonii.

areas; through a path of ponds or raised planting beds; or among found objects, topiary, or an unusual collection of vegetation. Let me guide you on a short trip through my garden to see how this works.

Departing from my kitchen door, we'll walk along a path toward our first destination: a 10-foot-high morning glory arch. On a rainy day the arch is a focal view from my kitchen window, but when the sun is out we can travel down the brick-and-blue-tile path, noting yellow and blue plantings of columbine, salvia, delphinium, nasturtium, and Siberian iris.

At the arch, rest your hand on a waist-high raised planter capped with blue tiles. Pause to inhale the fragrance of 'Stargazer' lilies. Notice that supports for the arch are made of copper that mirrors the brown tones of the leaves and bark of nearby weeping crabapple trees. Musical notes detailed in the copper evoke a story of my wedding ceremony held here, when we toasted our friends to favorite music.

Underneath the arch, gaze up into a canopy of mixed conifers, which supports a starry roof of *Clematis montana* var. *rubens,* a very reliable bloomer. Like the morning glory vine that inspired the design for the arch, the clematis has grown beyond its copper support to climb toward the sky.

A radiant yellow light draws us through the arch toward our next destination in a far corner of the garden. A planting of yellow tulips glows like globes of light. We've found my secret garden, hidden behind a wall of greenery. This destination

---

★★★★★★★★★★★★★★★★★★★

Tip: Plant Shovels to Locate Focal Points

Purchase six or seven inexpensive shovels. Paint the handles in different colors.

Take your shovels out into your garden and randomly "plant" them, digging them into the earth. Now stand back and see whether they mark good spots for features.

Ask yourself, "Is this a good place for something?" You don't need to know what that something is, you only need to have the feeling that something goes there. You are looking for a feeling of flow or direction of movement from one space to another.

The nice thing about the shovels is that you can keep moving them around until you feel that each of them is in a place where something will go.

Note the final locations of the shovels in your notebook. You are building up the shape and flow of focal points in your garden space.

★★★★★★★★★★★★★★★★★★★

invites us to sit on yellow stools shaped like water lily pads, resting among the yellow flowers next to a ceramic and metal fountain. Here we can pause to enjoy the chattering of birds perched among the branches overhead.

From our tour, you can see that my garden unfolds as a series of pathways leading to destinations. Each destination has its own unique reward: a blue petal bench enveloped in pink flowers, a fountain made of a mural showing women watering, a planter of bright colors sprouting a trellis, a painted wooden table where a foursome can eat lettuces, figs, and berries gathered from the garden.

Destinations serve multiple functions. For instance, in my garden the copper arch:

- ✳ Makes a gateway to a hidden area in the garden
- ✳ Focuses the view from my kitchen window
- ✳ Brings the color and texture of copper into the garden, enhancing awareness of the tree bark and leaves of a nearby weeping crabapple
- ✳ Repeats the natural imagery of the overhead morning glories
- ✳ Supports a large clematis vine
- ✳ Introduces musical imagery that offers a conversation starter for garden visitors
- ✳ Adds height to the surrounding layering of plants

It may sound fanciful, but organizing your garden as the map of a journey through your dreams will transform it into a destination where your dreams can come true. I've believed in the power of gardens to make dreams come true ever since childhood.

Left: *Keeyla's garden with copper morning glory arch supporting* Clematis montana *var.* rubens.

Right: *Painted blue petal bench with* Rosa 'Felicia' *on fence.*

Elevations

Forget flat! You can transform a small, flat space into a dynamic event by varying the elevations. Use raised planting beds, rock outcroppings, and dirt mounds to elevate garden spaces. I must confess that I revel in dirt. Building up one area and excavating another is my idea of heaven on earth. You too can learn to be a sculptor in your garden!

Have fun working the soil, moving it around, and trying new shapes. Let the activity of playing with dirt bring out the artist in you. Make mounds from dirt you had planned to cart off or that's left from digging out a pond, and top it with good soil. If your garden slopes away at the back, this is an opportunity to build it up. Mound, excavate, frolic in the dirt. Surrender to the warmth of an afternoon spent shaping your own heaven on earth.

Below: *California poppies and* Nemophila *baby-blue-eyes between placed rocks.*

Below right: *Carex and daffodil border.*

Far right: *Glazed tile and lily-pad stools surrounded by planted raised beds.*

Tip: Rock 'n' Roll in the Garden

If you are looking for fresh inspiration for your garden earthworks, take a drive and admire the shapes and habits of the land in your region. Notice how gravity pulls down skirted fans of silt, leaving nubby ridges of weathered cliffs. See how rock rubble collects at the base of hills and water seeps out of valleys.

In nature, rocks find their resting place with the help of gravity. So, when placing rocks in your garden, imagine where they would sit if the forces of gravity were moving them.

I have found that placing rocks in groups of three, with at least one large rock in the group, creates a natural effect. I also use triangular arrangements. I can't tell you why this works, but following my intuition has taught me that putting rocks in triangles and groups of three with one big rock consistently produces a pleasing arrangement.

At the end of the day, stand back and admire your work. Modify it if you like, or wait until morning for another look. You can easily revise and try new ideas until the shapes and heights feel just right. When you are ready to finalize your results, add planting soil and place rocks or boulders around the mounds for support before planting.

One of the many ways of adding elevations to your garden is by incorporating rocks or boulders. These natural sculptures, with their unique shapes and wonderful textures—sharp and angular or smooth and round—epitomize organic shapes.

Raised Planting Beds

Raised beds, planters, and mounds all make a garden more eventful and increase the sense of space. The raised planting beds toward the rear of my garden help to bring the flowers up to eye level and are like vases holding flowers from spring to fall.

A carpenter friend constructed the retaining walls for my raised beds out of wood. I watched him build the walls, following the same steps as for an ordinary fence: setting the posts in cement, nailing on horizontal stringers, and then setting the vertical pickets. He used screws to attach the pickets, which is time-consuming but lasts longer than nails.

When it was time to paint, I wanted the wood grain to show through. So I didn't use a primer, although we painted a water sealant on the soil-contact side of the retaining wall.

Connectors

Connectors are what tie together garden destinations, focal features, and the house or street. Pathways are the most common connectors. Bridges are another option. Stairs can be used as a connector where there is a change in elevation.

To get fresh ideas for laying out your paths, take yourself on what I call a "garden date." Go to the bookstore to look at paths in garden magazines and books. Perhaps buy one. Take a closer look over lunch. Walk around your neighborhood. Look at the paths. Are there shapes or materials that are unique to your local area?

Because pathways and connectors are basically lines, I suggest that you delve into the idea of lines. Look at how artists use lines in drawings, paintings, and sculpture. Choose a day to zoom in on lines as you go about your business, looking at billboards, signs, and clothing designs.

On my garden design map, connectors are the paths joining destination spaces, focal points, and the house, garage, and street. They appear as lines.

Left: *Daffodils and placed rocks.*

Right: *Pathway bordered by herb garden.*

Tip: Paint a Retaining Wall

Even though oil-based paints last longer than latex, I recommend latex because it spreads more fluidly and is easier to clean up.

Gather your painting materials in advance. You'll need:

- Drop cloth
- Latex or oil paints
- Several pairs of paint gloves
- Stirring sticks
- Rags for cleanup
- Paper buckets or used yogurt or milk containers

To allow the wood grain to show through, use a paint wash on bare wood. A paint wash is paint that has been thinned slightly to make it less viscous and more transparent. You can use either oil-based paint thinned with paint thinner or latex paint mixed with water.

Apply the paint with brushes, foam brushes, or rags.

I apply the paint with bristle or foam brushes and rub it in with rags so that the wood grain shows through. When the paint ages, spiff it up with a light sanding and reapplication of paint.

From a practical standpoint, some pathways are absolutely necessary: from the street to your front door or from your back door to a garage or shed. Other pathways are aesthetic designs serving both as paths and as visual cues to focal features.

Make copies of your garden map and experiment by drawing connectors. Have fun drawing the lines you saw on your garden date. Maybe instead of going directly to a garden destination, your path will be a winding journey, a spiral, or a writhing snake. Be aware that existing cement offers a sturdy surface on which to lay a path of brick, flagstone, or other material.

My garden is in an urban neighborhood with few natural features to relate to except the sky. The bayside sky above my garden is flirtatious, shifting from day to day—and during the day—through shades of blue and gray. The blues of the sky suggested a poetic mood, singing out the blues. In my poetic mood, I made blue ceramic path tiles, which I placed over an existing cement path.

Tip: Supporting Mixed Pavings

You'll need a sturdy base layer for your mixed paving. I use a pathway support material—a gravel product called "gray path fines," which is available at most construction or landscape outlets.

Mixed pavings can be laid over an existing area of concrete or brick and are a creative way to deal with ugly concrete surfaces. To get the paving surface level, put your thickest items down first. The top of your thickest material—flat rocks, pavers, or bricks—will determine the height of your paving. You can then use string and a carpenter's construction level to make sure that the rest of the materials are all at the same height. Put the gray path fines beneath all the other materials until they match the height of your thickest pieces.

Depending upon the desired effect, you can fill the spaces between your paving material with sand, moss, or more gray path fines.

Your mixed paving may be at or slightly below the surrounding soil level, but it will need a border to lock the pieces in place. I often use head-sized boulders to accomplish this. Once I found some discarded street-lamp parts that made a great perimeter for a mixed paving. See how creative you can be in finding border material.

You can also use raised beds as path borders, planted with perennials, annuals, bulbs, grasses, and shrubs.

Mixed Pavings

What is a mixed paving? It's a mixture of materials, such as rock, cobblestones, tile, and a variety of other flat or gravelly materials, combined to make a path, a patio, or a place to set a bench, a planter, or a sculpture.

I have several mixed paving areas in my garden. The wish to bring sky colors into my backyard inspired a mixed paving of brick, flagstone, rock, and glazed blue ceramic tiles. Later, I was told by a writer that the Portuguese call the blue tiles used in their pavings "eyes of the sky" or "eyes of the gods."

You can find many materials to combine into mixed pavings at building supply yards, quarries, and landscape material suppliers. I've seen tumbled glass used as gravel and old kitchen silverware on paths. One client of mine found the flagstones we used for a walkway too light in color, so we painted them with a paint wash. She liked them so much that we added more painted stones to the paving.

Below left: *Blue glazed tile mixed with flagstone and brick.*

Below: *Yellow tile and river-washed stones set on a sand base.*

Far left: *Glazed ceramic tile interplanted with ajuga, isotoma, Irish moss, and pink strawberries.*

Below left: *Purple-flowering Campanula.*

Right: *Ceramic tile with crocuses.*

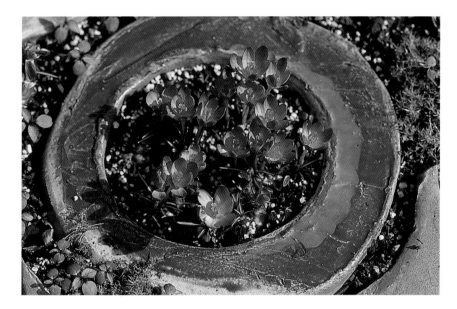

Taking mixed pavings even further, I made one that is a kind of painting on the ground. I fired and glazed ceramic pieces, placing them with a collection of ground cover plants that match the glazes. The piece, which I call "Butterfly Couple," has two heads and other parts loosely arranged to represent butterfly wings and bodies. The purple glazes of the ceramics match little purple pea flowers of Kenilworth ivy, the lime greens link up with Scotch moss, and the pinks pair with strawberry plants that have pink blooms. When viewed from the vantage point of a nearby deck, the ground cover and ceramic come together in a "ground painting."

Dry Creeks

Dry creeks are my favorite connectors for dividing and defining space. A dry creek looks like a winter creek that has dried up for the summer. They can vary in length and width, but their beds are strewn with rocks of varying sizes, and the banks that rise along their sides can be planted with grasses and wildflowers, depending on the look you want to achieve. They flow naturally onto a patio or into a meadow.

The top of a dry creek is a wonderful spot for a piece of sculpture or a container planted with flowers, because your eye is drawn up the creek. In my garden the creek bed is filled with smooth pebbles that have a purple hue to them. At the top I placed a pot glazed with lavender and bright yellow. The flowers, pot, and creek pebbles harmonize well. Mingled with the pebbles are stepping stones that draw children to them like magic. They love jumping from one to another up to the top of my dry creek.

In a dry creek, you're mimicking in the garden what nature leaves behind: exposed stones where winter rains no longer run over rocky rubble in a hillside crevice. The warm stones attract lizards and butterflies. A large rock in the creek bed makes a tempting spot to sit contemplating nature on a sunny afternoon or to share with a dragonfly.

Keep in mind the colors of any features that you're adding to the creek, such as large boulders, sculptures, or pots. I suggest choosing a color palette keyed to features that will enhance the colors of the creek elements. A rock creek is an ideal place to use unusual and colorful rocks. They turn the whole creek into a color expression.

Below: *Mixed paving of flagstone, Mexican black stones, cobbles, and gold path fines.*

Right: *Dry creek of mixed rocks planted with grasses and foxgloves.*

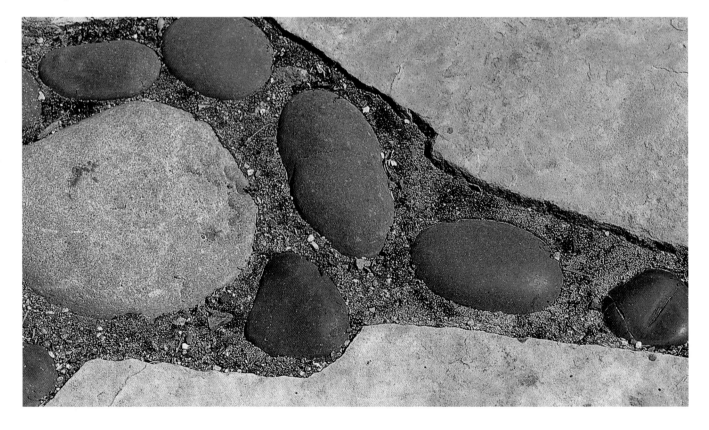

Tip: Take a Walk on the Wild Side: Making a Dry Creek

Dry creeks present a fun and easy opportunity to try your hand at mixing materials.

1. Gather a mixture of water-washed stones of various sizes and shapes:

   - Small, head-sized boulders
   - Rounded stones
   - Flat stones
   - Angular stones
   - Large cobbles
   - Pebbles

2. Along a flat or sloped surface, mark the path of your creek with string or spray paint.

3. Decide how wide your dry creek will be. I suggest making it between $2^{1}/_{2}$ feet and 5 feet wide.

4. Clear out the creek's path to get the desired length, width, curves, and bends.

5. Excavate 4 to 6 inches, mounding up the removed dirt along the sides.

6. Along the creek path, lay down weed-block cloth, available at landscape retail outlets.

7. To give your dry creek definition, make the outer walls of your creek as bold as you can manage, placing the chunkiest boulders along the sides and a few smaller rocks in the middle. In the center of your creek, pour some of the smaller pebbles, followed by larger stones and another layer of small pebbles.

8. Fill the crevices with your stones and pebbles.

9. The top of the creek is an excellent spot for placing a focal feature: a fountain, large container, or sculpture.

10. Natural plantings of grasses and bulbs work especially well as creekside boundaries and can attract butterflies and birds.

The main garden features I consider placing at garden focal points are fountains, sculptures, benches, planted containers, and trellises—although focal features can also be unusual trees or shrubs, specimen plants, large rocks, arbors, arches, or light fixtures. Focal features don't need to be as elaborate as sculpture: Almost any ordinary garden object, such as a bench, container, or gate, will do the trick. If you paint, decorate, or otherwise shape it into something unique, it will bring focus to the selection of materials for the connected space.

In "red lady" Laura's garden, for instance, the orange blades of stipa and carex, along with Peruvian lilies, mirror the tones of both boulders and a large metal sculpture. The surface patterns of

garden features: bringing focus to the garden

stones in the dry creek leading up to the sculpture resonate with the pounded texture of the sculpted copper tree.

Preceding pages, left to right: *Planted pot with yellowtwig dogwood and chrysanthemums backed by red wall. Shirley poppy.* Helichrysum *'Limelight'.*

Left: *Bronze shovel with dahlia and* Canna *'Tropicana'.*

Below: *Aloe and* Sedum *'Casablanca'.*

Right: *"Butterfly Bench" with dahlias.*

The idea of focal features is central to my gardening methods. So let's explore this idea further by returning to our departure point for this book: making gardens works of art. I've adopted a gardener's orientation to making artworks, both in and out of the garden.

I find that I really give my artist's cap a workout in the garden when creating focal features. As with a painting, I want to find what it is that each garden has to say. Does the garden want to say "nature"? If so, I would use mainly organic imagery, such as the colors of the leaves and bark of the surrounding trees. In Carmel near the Pacific Ocean, a garden feature could address the ocean with a partially buried whale fountain. The whale head would spout water, while its tail would emerge from a bed of native sea-blue penstemon.

A more architectural garden might speak in squares of glass and steel set against circular beds of architecturally compatible plants such as palms, cactus, or weeping conifers. Other gardens might speak in colors, such as an abstract color statement in copper and orange that engages light and shadow on painted walls.

If I'm stuck and can't figure out what a garden has to say, I will turn to the surrealist guerrilla tactics I learned in art school. One of these strategies is simply to open a dictionary to a word. Let's say I'm working in a small, tight space that I'd like to feel more expansive. I open my dictionary to a word . . . "line" is what I get. Hmmm, that gives me ideas. I love to play with lines in drawings. So I'm thinking, "Maybe this garden wants to speak in line drawings that go upward into the sky."

The sky is the limit when it comes to designing focal features. One thing leads to another in the garden, and each feature will engender another as you and your garden grow together. Spots where I started with just a plant or a simple feature now have planters with trellises, sculptures, rocks, and yet more distinctive plants. Some features have stayed the same for years; others have evolved and changed.

A good focal feature gives definition to the color and texture palettes of the surrounding area, focusing it into a unified composition. This incidentally makes a garden highly photogenic: It gives it a central focus with a harmonious surrounding. A single feature can define the design of just a section or a whole garden, and it will attract you and your friends out into the garden. The challenge is to combine the functional with the artistic in your garden.

A tall feature will direct attention up, while a low one will do the opposite, so consider what you want to draw attention to. If you have a neighboring view that you want to avoid, put a feature somewhat in front of it, and plant trees and shrubs behind the feature. This directs attention away from the unwanted scene.

Tip: Planting Shovels to Choose Focal Features

We have planted shovels as a way of discovering a garden's focal points. To decide what features to use in the focal points, let's return to planting shovels in the garden.

Write on slips of paper or note cards all of the features you might want in your garden. Include two types of items:

- The practical things you want in your garden, such as a sandbox, picnic table, barbecue, storage shed, mailbox, or other items

- Visual accents such as sculpture, a large container, a fountain, an artistic bench, an arch, a trellis, or a pond

Before you plant your shovels, divide the note cards into two stacks: practical features and artistic features.

Locate or replant your shovels at your focal points.

Once the placement of the shovel feels right, ask yourself, "What goes here?"

Choose the card for that feature, and tape it to the shovel. Work with your shovels and cards until each feature that you want in your garden is assigned to a shovel. Some of these features, such as a bench, will be destinations that you travel to. Others, such as a fountain, may be ones that you see from a kitchen window when working at a sink.

In art, this relation between foreground and background is called the figure/ground relationship. These relationships are central to painting, and they are especially useful in garden design.

For me, locating the right spot for features in the garden is an intuitive process. It starts with a flash of enthusiasm or inspiration: a moment that is planted like a seed and then protected, nurtured, and brought wondrously to fruition.

Fountains

I was amazed when I visited Rome. There were fountains everywhere! In Rome fountains are a passion. I don't understand why we Americans don't have more fountains in public or private spaces. The Romans also aren't shy about their love of sculpture. It is in the streets, restaurants, houses, and cafes. They mix sculpture with water and get . . . fountains. When it comes to fountains, I say, "Do as the Romans do." Put fountains in the street, in the parking lots, in your garden, or in your house.

The ingredients for a fountain are easy to find and work with. The hardware needed for making fountains is widely available at nurseries and better hardware stores. Most fountains require some fiddling to get them flowing right, but the results are worth it. Construction and installation may require technical assistance.

You need a pump, plastic tubing, and an extension cord to go to an electrical outlet. Be careful when working with electricity! Follow instructions and observe safety warnings.

A fountain might be as simple as a stone with a hole drilled through it or a plastic pipe that sends water trickling through a pile of rocks. Fountains add music and the many pleasures of water to the garden, attracting hummingbirds, dragonflies, and damselflies. The first pot fountains I made were hard to maintain because they had complicated tops. For a while I thought I'd give up on fountains, but I'm finding that they are much easier if I keep the plumbing simple. Now I just have a hose that leads directly from the pump sealed in the bottom of the pot up to the lid of the pot. Regular maintenance is still required to keep the fountains going.

I've made several vertical flat fountains. Flat fountains work very well against walls and are welcoming at a house entrance, either inside or out.

I have recently graduated from making ceramic fountains to creating fully sculptural fountains in bronze. For a long time, my desire to make fountains in bronze was like a seed inside me, waiting to germinate. It was cultivated by viewing the Matisse series *The Back,* as well as by seeing Bernini's monumental bronze

Left: *Painted shovel "planted" near* Stipa arundinacea.

Above: *Sculpture detail of cut glass and metal.*

Tip: Splish Splash Concerto: Get in Touch with Water Sounds

When considering a fountain, learn to tune in to the sounds that water makes. In an urban area you can find public fountains or listen to fountains at nurseries. Visit friends or neighbors who have fountains, and really *listen* to the water. Or even record it.

On a nature outing, you can listen to water sounds of all kinds. Think about the particular kind of sound you want in your garden. Do you need to disguise the noise of traffic with the roar of a waterfall or gather birds to sing with the gentle notes of a spring?

Play with the sounds that water makes. Turn on the garden hose and let it run into a bucket of water. Bring an assortment of materials into your garden for a splish splash concerto: rocks, wood, kitchen pans, pottery, even the kitchen sink. Have several containers that you can fill and pour from. Notice how the sound changes as you pour from a higher or lower position.

Take notes on the distance that water falls. If it falls from a very high place, the wind might blow it away. I found this out the hard way! But you can learn from my mistake.

Left: *Bronze fountain "Large Woman Watering."*

Above right: *Plumbing on fountain.*

Right: *Clay model for bronze fountain "Large Woman Watering."*

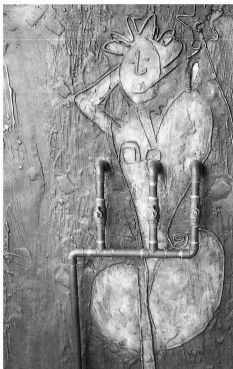

fountains during my travels in Italy. I felt the seed rumbling to get my attention. When I found a bronze foundry near where I live in Berkeley, the seed took root.

But still I dawdled, not knowing where to start, until one day I grabbed one of my ceramic garden pieces and had it cast in bronze. Since then, I have made giant morning glories, whimsical garden divas, bawdy couples, and my *pièce de résistance*, *Large Woman Watering*, all cast in bronze. My seed has sprouted, grown, and blossomed. It was quite a challenge!

If you feel a similar seed of desire inside you, seek out sculpture classes in your area. Start with a medium you feel comfortable with—even papier-mâché or play dough will do—but proceed with caution. You could end up with a monumental fountain in your own backyard!

Sculpture

As a pioneer in the trend toward bringing sculpture into the garden, I believe that sculpture in the home garden opens a gate to wider imagination, offering new ways to mix plants with such materials as glass, metals, ceramics, and even unusual lights.

As with anything else, the key to sculpture is practice and experience. Many classes and workshops are offered these days to help you get started in woodworking, metalcraft, glasswork, and clay. Your garden is a good place to practice these arts.

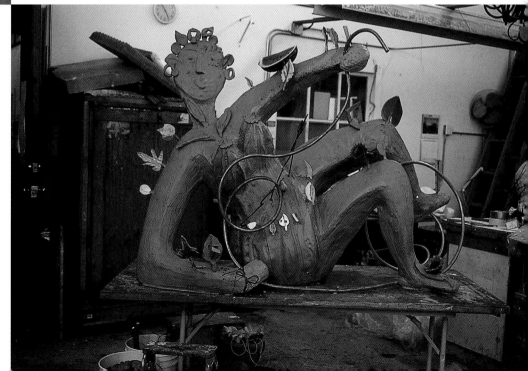

The San Francisco Bay Area has a lot of artists who make "art cars"—cars decorated with collections of found objects. One of my favorite art cars is covered in old cameras. For ideas, look around your city for people doing assemblage art. Scavenging for discarded objects at garage sales or flea markets and assembling them into works of art is great fun.

Below: *Painted shovels and aluminum tubing.*

Right: *Ceramic and metal sunflower.*

Below right: *Ceramic and metal sunflowers in front of painted wall.*

Like harmony and contrast, simplicity and complexity are also part of your design vocabulary to play with and to support you in making garden art. My sculptures have complex organic surfaces that resonate with rocks, layers of leaves, and shifting garden light. Left to my own devices, I tend toward complex designs. I respond to the complex patterns of butterfly wing markings, variegated foliage, intricate flower colorings, and the layered surface textures of rocks and moving water. On a spectrum of simple to complex, my work is at the very complex end of the scale. Once in a while, however, I will make something simple, such as a giant crayon fountain.

I stay away from judgments when it comes to simple versus complex. Complex gardens can be judged as cluttered and "a mess," while simple ones can be criticized as boring and "anal." The point in creating your own paradise on earth is that you get to decide what ignites your passions, soothes your soul, and assists in your growth. I recommend that you accept your taste and explore the possibilities.

For example, if you like complexity, try clustering several shapes together to make a sculpture. Try stacking the shapes up like a totem pole. You can increase the complexity by texturing the surface with a variety of materials or by adhering small objects. I often embed collections of things such as seashells or marbles in the surface of sculptures. If you like simplicity in design, try putting just one shape in a large, open space and possibly repeating that shape. It could be a simple square, an orb, or a pear shape.

The architecture of a house will direct you toward simple or complex designs. Contemporary architecture, with its sleek lines, invites sparse design. On a contemporary patio, I could set a collection of objects on posts to cast their shadows onto colored walls. On the other hand, a cottage can handle an all-out explosion of plants and sculptures. I could see surrounding a cottage with tall sunflower sculptures and a collection of whirligigs.

Sculpture and Grasses: A Match Made in Heaven

The relationship between plants and sculpture is dynamic and interactive, with the sculpture and the plants coming together in one field. A common way of working with plants and sculpture in the garden is to frame the sculpture with a neutral background of plants. This highlights the sculpture while the plants recede into the background.

Grasses call out to sculpture to join them in the garden. Bunch grasses that form clumps, and rediscovered western native grasses, are effective frames for

Left: *Copper and glass sculpture "Tree Form."*

Below: *Bronze sphere.*

Right: *Abutilon flower matching the coral tones of a painted bench.*

sculpture. Most of these grasses naturally have a color palette that is similar to metals such as copper and bronze or iron and steel as they age—ranging from tangerine, apricot, and saffron through rust and sepia.

The carexes in particular just seem to "plant" sculptures and metal furnishings in garden spaces by creating a textured field. They are stable and easy to work with, and they look good year-round.

I love how the seed heads and blades of a multitude of grasses play with wind and light. Abstract forms jut up easily from a clump of grasses. Sculpture can be like an abstract or impressionist painting, in which the plants, rocks, tables, and chairs come together to form a whole.

Bunch grasses are also a great foil to contrast against flowering perennials, bulbs, and wildflowers. Their textures move the eye easily. In addition, they attract birds, wildlife, and butterflies into your garden.

Benches

Benches make great focal features, beckoning you to sit and contemplate the garden from a fresh vantage point. I put at least one bench—and often several—in
every garden.

I consider them a friendly feature to place because they can be moved at will.
An inexpensive bench can easily be transformed with paint.

Benches have always been part of garden furnishings, and you can easily find
antique benches with lots of character or cast-off garage-sale benches ready for
rejuvenation. Prices range from free to very expensive, highly crafted pieces. I've
been given many benches over the years, keeping some and giving others to
neighbors.

My neighbor Jody simply repainted in plum purple a bench that I gave her. It
looked so good that I jokingly told her I wanted it back. But she just sat on it
and dared me to take it! Because they're cheap and easy to find, benches make
good garden features for experimentation.

Most of my bench designs have followed leaf and flower petal forms, and I've
found great satisfaction enlarging plant forms to make benches. I've found that
carpenters are eager to try their hand at realizing unconventional designs based
on natural forms. You too can draw inspiration from nature for bench designs.

Tip: Paint a Pot

Painting containers is a good way to unify your
garden composition. It's a small but rewarding garden project. Gather your painting materials:

- Drop cloth
- Latex paints
- Several pairs of paint gloves
- Stirring sticks
- Oil pastels
- Pencil
- Paper scissors
- Rags for cleanup
- Paper buckets or used yogurt or milk containers
- Various combs or brushes
- Utensils to make designs in the paint
- Leaves or sketched designs

To make sure your pot is completely free of moisture, keep it inside for a few days before you paint.
Likewise, let the paint dry well before you plant in
the pot. Moisture will make your paint bubble,
blister, and peel.

However, I've had the paint blister and yet still
look good for years. Mistakes are often perfectly
usable in the garden.

Start with a light wash as an undercoat. A paint
wash is paint that has been thinned slightly to
make it less viscous and more transparent.

Then apply a textured layer—this very simple
method is quite appealing. I apply paint in every
conceivable way: dripping, brushing, or splattering.
You can make a dynamic color texture by first
applying one color and letting it dry. Then apply the
second coat with rags, crumpled newspaper, or
sponges. You can also run a comb or brush through
the wet second layer of paint to reveal a bright
color beneath.

An easy way to start a bench design is to photocopy or scan a bench from a magazine or catalog. Then superimpose organic shapes on it—taping or drawing leaf and flower patterns onto it and indicating which shapes form the seat, back, legs, and armrests.

You can blend practically any bench or design into your garden with paint, selecting colors that harmonize or contrast with existing colors in the garden. Or your bench could be a starting point for a new planting. What would happen if you picked wild vermilion or bright turquoise colors for a bench? What would you plant with it?

Yet another idea is to collect toys and bric-a-brac from flea markets and garage sales—anything that will tolerate outdoor weather, such as old garden tools, bottle caps, marbles, and tin signs. (Avoid sharp objects.) Attach this collection to your bench, using nails, screws, glue, or wire. It could even be a family or neighborhood project. If you completely cover a bench to the point that you can no longer sit on it, you have a garden sculpture!

Containers

Just a single container can make an inspiring work of art. Containers make perfect focal features; I use them in every garden I design. By extending the color palette of the container and its planting into your selection of vegetation and stones, you can more clearly define an area and make it more appealing as a whole.

Again, take your design cues from the architecture of the house. Try all sorts of containers. Many wonderful Asian planters are available, as well as that old standby, terra-cotta pots. There are ceramic, cement, and wooden containers for every garden situation. Place a collection of pots around a bench to bring guaranteed admiration from friends. A bench flanked by pots is a tried and true focal arrangement for small gardens.

Most of my own planters are handmade ceramic vessels that are glazed and fired. You can get the same brilliant colors by painting terra-cotta, cement, or wooden planters.

Trellises

Bare branches are one of my favorite inspirations from the garden. I never tire of looking at them, and I respond to almost any artwork with branches in it.

One thing that many gardeners have in common is a love of branches. They are poetic when bare and covered in snow, dripping with rain, showing translucent

Left: *Painted bench with ceramic figs next to fig tree.*

Above: *Pot with lemon tree branches and woman with petal hairdo.*

green leaves, heavy with fruit, or bejeweled with the fiery leaves of autumn.

Constructing trellises from wood and branches was my first attempt at making artistic features for the garden. Materials for making trellises are easily available and inexpensive: branches, wood slats, twine, wire, and nails. You can start with these materials and then add personal touches later. I love seeing flowering vines as well as peas and beans from the vegetable garden winding their way up a trellis.

My first paintings were "trellis paintings." I actually made trellises for my paintings at the same time I was making garden trellises.

As an artist, it was comforting to discover that I could make art in the same way that I gardened. It took all of the residual expectations left over from art school out of the process and put the simple passion of gardening into making art.

When making a trellis, let it be fun. Experience the flow of improvisation, following ideas as they come up. Let the materials or the garden speak to you.

Among the harvests of fall are the piles of tree prunings that litter yards and sidewalks. Be on the lookout for ways to work branches into your artful garden.

Look in the stores where you purchase your containers for possible trellis materials. Try adding a sculptural trellis to a pot to support a vine, shrub, or small tree such as dogwood, weeping birch, or standard wisteria. I was amazed at how many vines and roses I could stuff into a pot to make a fountain of foliage and flowers climbing up and cascading from a supporting decorative trellis. I combine bamboo rakes and ladders with Asian pots to distinctively highlight twining vine foliage.

Left: *Copper-covered branch trellis with 'Gold Heart' ivy.*

Above: *Glazed ceramic pot with painted steel trellis and Parrot tulips.*

Right: *Glazed pot with* Euphorbia *'Sticks on Fire'.*

afterword

Part of becoming an artist in your garden is practicing the art of enjoying the fruits of your labor. After the work of creating your paradise, give yourself time to acknowledge and celebrate what you've done.

There are so many ways to receive pleasure from a garden. Sketch with colored pencils in your garden notebook. Photograph your garden or record its sounds. Sit on your newly painted bench. Savor the rich colors of the flowers, leaves, twigs, and berries. Inhale the fragrance of plants and the soil itself. Feel the sun, air, and light. Notice the change of seasons. However you choose to be in your garden, appreciate the bounty it has to offer.

My garden has given me the courage and vision to create things that I never imagined were possible in my life. Let your garden support you and encourage new avenues of discovery and creativity. When a project comes to fruition—like a bed of flowers in bloom, a sculpture or fountain nestled into its setting, or ripe fruits and vegetables ready for picking—celebrate with the people around you—and celebrate with yourself.

Happy Gardening!
Keeyla Meadows

Left: *Glazed ceramic and copper "Women Watering" fountain.*

Gardeners, like cooks, need to know their ingredients. A good gardener knows the plants of a region and their seasonal changes just as a good cook knows the seasons of the local produce. After a while, the rhythms of a place are in your blood.

I love to climb a street near my house in spring, when the acacia trees don their cloaks of yellow foam, welcoming a new season of leaves, blooms, fruits, and berries. For me, the acacia trees, along with nearby flowering magnolias, ornamental plums, and cherry trees, are the essence of spring. The local natives put on a show as well, and one of my

Far left: *California poppies.*
Left : *Dogwood twig.*
Above: *Dahlia.*

an annotated list of keeyla's favorite plants

favorites, the native dogwood *Cornus nuttallii,* offers the brightest welcome to the joys of spring.

trees

Left: Dogwood, *Cornus* species.

When planting gardens, I consider the native trees and plants first. After that, I am eager to try new species. We gardeners are often trying to expand what we know will do well in our gardens, even when a tree or shrub we fall in love with doesn't quite fit the neighborhood or climate. I know I'm guilty of lusting after the black-and-white painted bark of aspens, although my Bay Area climate isn't cold enough for them. Over the years, however, I've gleaned sufficient common sense from failed experiments that I stick to using plants that fit the weather and soil conditions of a particular environment.

I'm always on the lookout for plants with artistic colors, textures, and shapes. I offer here a sampling of plants—from the tallest trees to the flattest of ground covers—that have caught this artist's eye. In my accompanying notes, I focus on the plants' artistic uses. Browse through this list for ideas that can contribute to making your garden a wonderful work of art.

Needless to say, some of these plants may not be adapted to your region or conditions. Check your local nursery, reference books, or the Internet for information on each plant's cultural requirements.

1. Weeping contorted birch, *Betula pendula* 'Contorta'

This tree is a showstopper. It works very well as a focal feature, especially when its pendulous branches are draped over naturally carved rock. Like most weeping trees, this one does well in large containers that are at least 2 feet in diameter and depth. I find that weeping trees offer wonder and interest throughout the season.

2. Weeping bronze beech, *Fagus sylvatica* f. *purpurea*, f. *pendula*

I call this small, low-growing tree a dainty dancer, and I want front row seats for her seasonal performances. Her curtains of yellow-gold leaves and her milk chocolate–colored branches will keep you entertained from spring through winter.

This tree does well in planters or in the ground. You can easily find both tall specimens and short ones. Place this tree along one of the paths you travel daily.

3. Dogwood, *Cornus* species

Blooming pink or white, dogwoods are a perfect small tree for diminutive gardens. They don't take up too much space and are easily pruned to stay about 8 to 12 feet high. I use dogwoods in containers with roses climbing up their slim trunks. From a distance, dogwood flowers look like giant snowflakes suspended in air, offering artistic design inspiration for benches or planters. Dogwoods do well as an understory to larger trees, either deciduous or coniferous. Some regions have native dogwoods, which are a wonderful but often temperamental addition to the garden.

4. Chinese pistache, *Pistacia chinensis*

This tree is grown for summer shade and fall color. It's often used as a street tree. After we painted my client Laura's house in bold reds, greens, and golden yellows, we were delighted in fall when the huge pistache on her front lawn joined the color party, matching perfectly the saturated hues of the house.

5. Madrone, *Arbutus* species

I'm mad about madrones. The smooth, sensuous, red-brown outer bark and green inner bark are valuable threads for a garden tapestry. The colors of madrone bark blend especially well with the earthy salmons often painted on Mediterranean-style houses, while suggesting a flower palette of salmon oranges and coral pinks. On the West Coast madrones are a valuable native tree that can work in a stark and rugged landscape of rock and manzanitas. Multitrunk varieties offer quick salvation for abandoned slopes. For native plant enthusiasts, they offer year-round stability in color and form, providing shade for a swath of native blue wildflowers.

Right: Madrone, *Arbutus* species.

shrubs

Left: Snowy River wattle, *Acacia boormanii.*

Shrubs are a foliage lover's ticket to paradise, and they excite my appetite for the unusual. You can find shrubs with foliage, stems, and bark in every plant color and in every imaginable shape and texture.

When making your garden a work of art, use shrubs as the backdrop for your garden painting. They can form hedges behind plantings of flowers. Repeating one type of shrub in a line or group makes a strong color statement—along a driveway, for instance, or forming a living fence between neighbors.

Choose shrubs for their foliage color; they needn't be boring "wallflowers." Blossoming shrubs give the effect of a fountain of flowers. Spiraeas, hydrangeas, and several viburnums will burst into bloom like waterfalls showering blossoms. Plant highly fashionable shrubs such as edgeworthias, witch hazels, bronze sambucus, or 'Winter Fire' cornus in wildly painted pots for frighteningly modern focal features. Find a shrub with an unusually colored berry or with stickery stems and red foliage to become a partner in the garden alchemy of transforming some dull spot into a showstopper.

1. Purple smoke bush, *Cotinus coggygria*

Cotinus coggygria is a plant that interacts with and transforms in the light of the day and night. Its leaves shimmer when silhouetted in the glow of morning light. Its filaments of smoky seed pods point to the Milky Way at night.

This shrub is essential for artist-gardeners. Its stems and foliage are a striking palette of maroon-brown, bronze, and red-mahogany. Its color range, from purple/bronze to chartreuse green, can serve as a palette for a planter or an entire garden. Cultivars of this plant are available in several subtle shadings.

2. Elderberry, *Sambucus* species

Where did all these varieties of elderberry come from? There's a bronze one, a chartreuse one, a cutleaf one, and white and variegated types. I'm sure that there are also others I haven't had the pleasure of meeting yet. Wherever they came from, I'm glad they are here.

These shrubs are useful. All grow fast, so they are a quick fix for an unsightly wall or a hole in the back of a shrub border. Try mixing them in planters with grasses and lilies for a living summer bouquet. The flat-headed umbel blossoms look like fireworks and will be happy to climb up the trunk of a tree.

3. Rock rose, *Cistus ladanifer* 'Blanche'

'Blanche' is the largest girl in the cistus tribe. In my garden she reaches up to the top of a 12-foot portico, where she hangs out with 'Buff Beauty', a rose of an apricot color. Together they are quite a pair. 'Blanche' betrays my first rule of color: Don't mix white with other colors when you want a strong, brilliant palette. But 'Blanche' was there first, and I can't let her go. Her 4- to 5-inch white flowers bloom in early spring. I've also planted her quite successfully in deer territory, so apparently the deer don't mess with her either.

4. Redtwig dogwood, *Cornus stolonifera;* yellowtwig dogwood, *C. stolonifera* 'Flaviramea'

The winter coral-and-red twigs of *Cornus stolonifera* look as though they were on fire and deserve the name "twigs on fire," but it is already taken by an alarmingly orange euphorbia. One variety does claim the name 'Winter Fire' and, when it's grown as a companion to the coral bark maple, *Acer palmatum* 'Sango Kaku', the effect is a shockingly colorful trim for winter's often drab cloaks of brown. An elegantly variegated hybrid with lime-green and white leaves should relieve the monotony of European birch trees that grace so many front lawns.

5. Snowy River wattle, *Acacia boormanii*

This willowy member of the acacia family makes a fast-growing screen to hide neighborly indiscretions. Its palette of gray-green leaves and buds, red-brown bark, and frothy yellow flowers is earthy and artistic. It combines well with the bronze and rust tones of metal and glass in yellow or green. I've successfully grown it in containers, where the gray-green leaflets match the foliage of that grande dame of poppies, Ms. Matilija.

Right: Snowy River wattle, *Acacia boormani.*

perennials

Left: Anise hyssop, *Agastache foeniculum* 'Apricot Sunrise'.

Flowers will always be my chosen pathway to paradise. They are the sweetness of life, the brilliance that teases the imagination, and the joy that is a constant companion through the vagaries of this world. Flowers call the mythic goddess Persephone up from the underworld in spring. I can relate to that.

My list of favorite flowers is so long that it could fill a whole book. Apparently a lot of others feel the same way, for there are many wonderful catalogs featuring the world's treasure trove of flowers. I started my love affair with flowers by buying seeds from catalogs and then lining the railings on my back porch with seed trays. Growing flowers from seeds is easy and satisfying and less expensive than purchasing plants. There is no excuse for not having flowers.

This handful of flowers offers a mere hint of the bounty you have to choose from.

1. Peruvian lily, *Alstroemeria* species

Alstroemerias never cease to amaze me for their variety of warm colors. Their hues match and mingle well with the apricot- and coral-toned David Austin roses. They are also one of the best cut flowers. Plant them in the cutting garden, in containers, among tall grasses, and beneath sculpture with colored glass, glazed ceramic, or painted steel. These plants multiply rapidly. You can lift a group of their tubers from the ground to plant in another spot in the garden or to give to a friend.

2. Anise hyssop, *Agastache foeniculum* 'Apricot Sunrise'

Agastache is a newcomer to my plant repertoire. I find that it sways in the wind along with the grasses. Its tangerine shades harmonize with the browns of *Carex comans* or with other bronze-tinted foliage. It does quite well in a container planting on a patio, at a front entrance, or as a focal feature at one end of a dry creek.

3. Olympic poppy, *Papaver pilosum*

The soft orange of the papery petals is luscious, the coloring reminiscent of fresh-cut cantaloupe. The origin of this lovely poppy is Mount Olympus, and I'm sure it will please you as much as it does the gods who dwell there.

4. Avens, *Geum coccineum* 'Georgenberg'

Geum is a sizable species of perennials in apricot and orange colors that like to dance boldly in a front line bordering grasses. 'Georgenberg' has a piquant apricot color that combines with orange tulips in the spring, lending a hand in ventures along the sunny side of the color wheel. They are not particularly good as cut flowers, but geums can tolerate shade during part of the day, and so provide color in a semishady lawn area, particularly when mixed with red fescue.

5. Cinquefoil, *Potentilla* species

Because of the wide range of the potentillas, from coastal road-cuts to alpine mountaintops, I imagine that some form of this plant can be found in your area. I plant potentillas in meadow gardens, along with Pacific Coast iris and native grasses.

 I started with the bright yellow types, but I have found varieties with red flowers and gray leaves that can carry the gray foliage tones of tall shrubs, such as the red-flowering guava, down to the ground.

Right: Cinquefoil, *Potentilla* species.

annuals

Left: Nasturtium, *Tropaeolum* species.

Among my favorite annuals are California wildflowers: California poppy, godetia, phacelia, and nemophila. Like a Janey Appleseed, I scatter their seeds in the fall on top of bulb plantings, between trimmed-back perennials, and even along the city pathway where I walk in spring.

Collecting seeds both from the wild and from cultivated dry seedpods in the garden is high on my list of fun garden activities. I keep the seeds in labeled brown paper bags until it is time to sow them in the fall.

Last year's crop of flowers is a reliable source for next year's seeds. To separate red Shirley poppies from the pink ones, I tag the plant while it's blooming to know what color flower I have for the next year's planting.

1. Poppy, *Papaver* species

There are both perennial and annual poppies. Among the annuals, Shirley poppies *(Papaver rhoeas)* add red tones to tall plantings, and Iceland poppies *(Papaver nudicaule)* are an old favorite for interplanting with tulips and ranunculus to make a garden bouquet.

All poppies are easy to grow. They prefer sun, self-sow, and rebloom when cut back. Also, most varieties require little water. I sow poppy seeds in the fall. Rough up the soil on natural banks with a shovel, pick, or rake, and then toss out about a half inch of planting or Keeyla's Secret Soil Mix (see Tip on page 36) before scattering the flower seeds. You are guaranteed a landslide of flowers in the spring.

2. Baby-blue-eyes, *Nemophila menziesii*

Baby-blue-eyes is another easy-to-grow annual. Cast the seeds in the fall, following the same instructions as for poppies. They thrive in partial shade. Baby-blue-eyes will cascade over the side of a pot as easily as over a rocky outcropping.

A variety called 'Baby Black Eyes' being sold in the Bay Area has black-and-white flowers. Look for seeds of this plant if you can't find it in a 4-inch container. The black-toned flowers point out darker tones in bronze sculpture, black marble, and granite stone pieces. They also contrast with a wide variety of colors, including pinks, salmons, whites, and light greens.

3. Sunflower, *Helianthus* species

Van Gogh brought sunflowers to our attention like no other artist. Sunflowers inspire whimsy, and a multitude of sunflower art is available through galleries, in catalogs, and at nurseries, waiting to link with your imagination to create a living garden picture. It's easy to get sunflower seeds to grow: Just till the soil and dump the seeds in. Sunflowers attract birds, squirrels, ants, and people, including painters and sculptors.

4. Nasturtium, *Tropaeolum* species

Nasturtiums are so easy to grow that they border on being considered weeds. The orange, red, salmon, yellow, and apricot colors are perfect for gaily painted pots, for trellises, and for cascading over brightly painted walls, climbing up to sit on the lap of a colorfully painted sculpted lady.

5. Toadflax, *Linaria reticulata* 'Flamenco'

At garden shows, this airy plant brings the most attention and questions. Growing to a height of about 16 inches, it is a short-lived perennial or an annual, depending on how cold your winters get. I grow it as an annual. It freely reseeds, bringing a cheery note among the cracks of pavement or hanging out of pots. Its candy-colored maroon-red and gold-yellow heads bob about in the breeze. The pouchy form of the flower heads reminds me of the puffy purses of *Calceolaria integrifolia* 'Golden Nugget'. The two would make happy companions sauntering along a garden walkway.

Right: Poppy, *Papaver* species.

ground covers

Ground covers are the last group of plants to go in when you are planting a whole landscape because they fill in the spaces between the larger perennials. They are also the final vegetation for filling in the cracks of a mixed paving; they make a comfortable transition from the hardscape materials of stone, cement, and brick to the softscape of plants and flowers. I find that ground covers combine well with hardscape materials to make sculptural effects right in a path. You can surround an artistic path paver made of glass, stone, brick, cement, or metal with ground covers for an intriguing moment of contemplation while you traverse a garden path.

1. Dymondia, *Dymondia margaretae*

This matting plant hugs the ground, making a great filler between patio and walkway pavers. The gray-green foliage sets off desert sunset–colored rocks and would make a perfect nest for some kind of giant sculpted garden egg.

2. Creeping mint, *Mentha requienii*

I plant creeping mint, or Corsica mint, in small patches for the fragrance. Rub your fingers over the leaves to enjoy an aromatic moment. Creeping mint could inspire the construction of a living seat or a corny rock sculpture to place in a shallow pot, with the mint as the hair of a carved garden gargoyle.

3. Carpet bugle, *Ajuga reptans* 'Catlin's Giant'

Like smaller ajugas, this giant one has good color and reliable performance. When you're weaving a palette of browns and purples, the ajugas are the low-growing threads in the tapestry.

Left: Thyme, *Thymus* species.

4. Thyme, *Thymus* species

Almost all drought-tolerant gardens use thyme to line walkways and edge borders. A reliable plant that comes in many forms and colors, it doesn't require too much water or care. Thyme benefits from a haircut after blooming or when unsightly woody growth takes over. The flowers attract bees, which is a plus for pollinating orchards but should be avoided at poolsides or in children's play areas.

5. Bellflower, *Campanula* species

Campanula was the first shade-loving ground cover in my plant repertoire when I began landscaping professionally years ago. It remains a tried-and-true member of my team. Available in purple and white, *Campanula poscharskyana* is an easy ground cover for the shaded garden. It appreciates soil renovation when planting and the reliable water of an irrigation system. *Campanula portenschlagiana* has a small leaf and deep purple flower; it is less vigorous but takes well to niches in vertical walls. *Campanula carpatica* 'Blue Clips' and 'White Clips' are my choices to plant in hanging baskets, set off a bronze sculpture, or mark the turn in a pathway heading for a cutting garden.

Right: Ceramic rock head and thyme.

grasses

Left: Mixed grasses.

Grasses define contemporary gardens. They are very linear but at the same time graceful, so they can ease the often hard lines of architecture or sculpture. Grasses smooth the transition between cultivated garden and grasslands or open space. They are at the heart of the wild garden and play a large role in reclaiming land for the birds, bees, and butterflies.

Many water-guzzling lawns would be better off replaced by native grasses and wildflowers. Check with your local native nurseries for species that are well suited to your conditions. Grasses open new doors for the garden artist.

1. Giant feather grass, *Stipa gigantea*

The brassy, yellow-gold plumes of *Stipa gigantea* call out to metal sculpture to join the band. As its name *gigantea* infers, this is a giant among grasses, so it should anchor the rear of a border. It combines well with the bronze members of the carex family and spotted tiger lilies.

2. Pheasant's tail grass, *Stipa arundinacea (Anemanthele lessoniana)*

In the garden, *Stipa arundinacea* and zauschneria sing together in a chorus of crimson and tangerine hues. Plant blue-handled shovels between the orange blades of *Stipa arundinacea* and you have instant garden art. In the summer, sow sunflower seeds to round out the picture.

3. Idaho fescue, *Festuca idahoensis*

Festuca idahoensis is a low-growing, clumping grass in hues that range from gray to blue; it plays well with blue wildflowers. In the fall, scatter a handful of baby-blue-eyes, love-in-a-mist, forget-me-nots, blue flax, and phacelia between its gray blades. By spring you will have a gentle patch of blues.

4. Red fescue, *Festuca rubra*

Festuca rubra can replace a lawn. The soft blades are inviting to lounge on. Planted down a hillside, it will guard against soil erosion, while making a waterfall of waving green. A contractor friend told me that this grass can be found in sod form for an instant carpet of green. Plant *Festuca rubra* among an outcropping of rocks for a meadow, tucking Pacific Coast hybrid iris into soil pockets between the rocks.

5. Berkeley sedge, *Carex* 'Tumicola'

I was surprised and pleased to hear that this grass is native to my region. It makes a verdant border that can invite swimmers down a path leading to pool or spa. Interplant with rare bulbs such as a collection of brodiaeas, camassias, or calochortus for a natural effect. Yellow wild ranunculus will fall all over this grass, in starry constellations of tiny yellow blooms.

Right: Rock 'n' roll with grasses and perennials.

bulbs

Left: Tulip, *Tulipa* species.

1. Tulip, *Tulipa* species

Tulips are at the top of the list for adding color to a gardener's paint box. Ranging from stark white to inky blue-blacks, tulips have cornered the color market for flowers. You can readily turn your garden into a color painting with tulips. When planted in groups of ten or more, they really "read" as a color. For this reason, tulips are very photogenic and worth the possibly large expense and trouble you may incur. I purchase them in September when they first arrive at the nurseries and then label, bag, and put them in the refrigerator until it's time to plant. The planting dates for tulips vary from region to region; check with your local nursery for the best time for your area.

My list of favorites keeps growing so that I now find myself planting at least five hundred tulips in my garden each year. Some of my favorites are the Viridiflora tulips 'Spring Green' and 'Greenland' (a green-and-pink tulip); 'Menton' (large-flowered and melon-colored); 'Fantasy' (a Parrot tulip that is marbled red-pink and green); 'Orange Bowl' and Fosteriana tulip 'Orange Emperor' (for orange); and 'Balalaika' (for red). I'm also very fond of the Darwin tulips 'Sweet Harmony' (creamy yellow) and 'Daydream' (pastel shades of apricot). Parrot tulips are best planted to droop over the edge of containers, for they have floppy stems. Peony tulips, with their multipetaled flowers, mass nicely in front of long-stemmed tulips such as 'Princess Irene'. This lovely orange-and-mahogany tulip is one of my favorites for fiery colors that interplant naturally with brown-toned grasses such as *Carex flagellifera*.

2. Daffodils, *Narcissus* species

I marvel at the variety of shapes and sizes of daffodils; they are real garden champions. Starting small, I like to plant the little hoop daffodil along a well-traversed path leading to a natural sweep of a hundred or more of the larger-flowering 'King Alfred', 'Carlton', or 'Giant Park' marching down a hillside.

3. Ranunculus

In bulb-planting classes, people often ask me which way to plant the spidery tubers of the Persian ranunculus. I hold up the bulb, or more accurately the tuber, with the spidery legs pointing down. Ranunculus are easy to interplant with other bulbs, annuals, or perennials because the tubers are so small. You need only to "slip" them beneath the earth for them to grow. One of my favorite planting combinations is ranunculus with tulips and Iceland poppies.

Ranunculus, along with poppies and columbine, have that airy, dancing quality typical of flowers with long thin stems and blooms that seem to float. I use all colors of ranunculus, combining white ones with greens, blues, and yellows, and red and purplish ones with burgundy and bronze foliage plants—most notably heucheras. My favorite ranunculus are those with salmon shades, which pick up some of my most brilliant glazes for containers.

4. African corn lily, *Ixia* species

Ixia and grasses are a match made in heaven. The foliage and flower stems of ixia are grasslike and graceful, saying yes to any dance offered by the wind. I prefer to buy ixia in separated colors, although it is easier to find them in a mix. The bulbs are small and more visible when you plant three to six bulbs in a single hole. The clumps multiply and can be dug up and divided to cover a greater area. The most readily available ixia are white with a dark eye, yellow, pink, and dark pink. There is also a turquoise ixia that is rare and hard to find but worth seeking out. It is a bit more tender than the others and might be best grown in a pot.

5. Lily

Lilies bloom in warm weather, so they are a part of the late spring and summer color palette for the garden. Aside from being strikingly beautiful, lilies help the artist gardener paint with flowers. There is a lily for each color palette, from casa blanca (white) to Antonia (pink), Citronella (yellow) to Tiger rose (salmon), Martigon (deep rose) to Stargazer (red-pink). I planted Stargazer in my garden at the base of the copper supports for the morning glory arch. The buds mimic the shapes of the pipes in the arch and the flower tones pick up the warm tones of the copper. The reds and pinks also harmonize with the mauve-painted wall below and contrast with the blue tile wall cap. As an adjunct to being so agreeable in helping me with my garden picture, Stargazer, like most lilies, perfumes the air and is great as a cut flower. I always plant lilies in groups of at least three, since a single stem looks gangly and awkward, and dig about a gallon of my Secret Soil Mix into the lily hole. Where there are root-eating critters, plant the bulbs in baskets. Surely a garden full of lilies sets the stage for a midsummer's night garden dream come true.

Right: Lily.

about the author

Born in San Fernando Valley among tumbleweed and acanthus bushes, Keeyla
Meadows moved as a child to a canyon above Beverly Hills—just up the street
from an old woman who would sit under an umbrella, selling maps to the homes
of the stars.

Keeyla has a B.A. from the California Institute of the Arts, where she studied
with John Baldisarri and Alan Kaprow. She earned her Masters Degree in
Sculpture at University of California at Berkeley, studying there with world-
renowned sculptor Peter Voulkous, with post-graduate studies at the Whitney
Museum of American Art.

For over twenty years, Keeyla has run a full-scale landscaping company, Keeyla
Meadows Gardens and Art, in the San Francisco Bay Area, where she also has a
gallery that shows her sculpture, paintings, furniture, and planters for the garden.
Keeyla's garden has appeared on *Good Morning America* and *Grow It!* television
programs. She teaches garden classes and lectures on garden topics at her home
and at local nurseries and garden events. She has published articles about color in
the garden in magazines and newspapers, and her garden has been featured in
numerous national magazines as well as in garden publications in Japan, Finland,
and England. She won the Best in Show Golden Gate Award at the 2001 San
Francisco Flower and Garden Show.